MYTH AND
HISTORY IN
CARIBBEAN FICTION

MYTH AND HISTORY IN

Caribbean Fiction

ALEJO CARPENTIER, WILSON HARRIS, AND EDOUARD GLISSANT

Barbara J. Webb

The University of Massachusetts Press

Amherst

Copyright © 1992 by
The University of Massachusetts Press
All rights reserved
Printed in the United States of America
LC 92–1356
ISBN 0–87023–784–5
Designed by Dorothy Thompson Griffin
Set in Plantin by Keystone Typesetting, Inc.

Library of Congress Cataloging-in-Publication Data
Webb, Barbara J., 1946–
Myth and history in Caribbean fiction : Alejo Carpentier, Wilson Harris, and
Edouard Glissant / Barbara J. Webb.
p.   cm.
Includes bibliographical references and index.
ISBN 0-87023-784-5 (alk. paper)
1. Caribbean fiction—History and criticism.   2. Carpentier, Alejo, 1904–
—Criticism and interpretation.   3. Harris, Wilson—Criticism and
interpretation.   4. Glissant, Edouard, 1928–   —Criticism and
interpretation.   5. Myth in literature.   6. History in literature.
7. Literature and history.   I. Title.
PN849.C3W4   1992
809.3′009729—dc20
92–1356
CIP

British Library Cataloguing in Publication data are available.

In memory of my brother Durant

and my father

Contents

CONTENTS

Acknowledgments

The research for this book was supported in part by grants from the National Endowment for the Humanities and the PSC/CUNY Research Award Program of the City University of New York.

It would be impossible to thank all the people who offered advice and assistance during my research in the Caribbean, but I wish to extend my sincere appreciation to the staff at Jamaica Institute and the faculty members of the University of the West Indies at Mona and St. Augustine for their warm welcome and help in countless ways. I am especially grateful to Edward Kamau Brathwaite, Mervyn Morris, Michael Dash, and Annette Insanally at the Mona campus in Jamaica; and Gordon Rohlehr, Earl Lovelace, and the former deputy librarian Barbara Comissiong at the St. Augustine campus in Trinidad for generously sharing their ideas and helping me locate research materials. I am forever thankful to Micheline and Daniel Maximin and their parents for making my stay in Guadeloupe and Martinique such a memorable and productive one. Thanks are also in order for the encouragement and hospitality of my friends Wally Look Lai of

Trinidad and María Cristina Rodríguez and Janice Gordils of the University of Puerto Rico.

My special appreciation goes to Dr. Wilfred Cartey, who first inspired my interest in comparative studies of Caribbean literature many years ago; and to Haydée Vitali and John Coleman, who encouraged my work in this area when I was a graduate student at New York University.

I am indebted to my friends and colleagues Soledad Romero and Ann Dobbs for reading my translations and offering helpful suggestions; Annick Piant for working with me on the Glissant translations; June Bobb for taking time to read the manuscript at various stages while carrying out her own work; and Ana Celia Zentella for always being such a good friend.

Many thanks to the readers and staff of the University of Massachusetts Press for their careful attention to the manuscript, and especially to Bruce Wilcox, the director of the Press, for his gracious support.

I thank my family and above all my husband, Wodajo Mogues, for his patience, understanding, and support during the long periods that this project took up so much of my attention.

MYTH AND HISTORY IN CARIBBEAN FICTION

Introduction

Modern writers often equate history with the much-maligned realism of traditional literature and reject historical representation in fiction in favor of what they consider the more creative forms of mythic discourse. Among Caribbean writers this issue is related to the generally negative perception of New World history as a legacy of dispossession, exploitation, and betrayal. In an effort to escape the alienating effects of that history, some Caribbean writers have turned to the archetypal patterns of myth. Thus the West Indian poet Derek Walcott opens his essay "The Muse of History" with the epigraph from Joyce: "History is the nightmare from which I am trying to awake." He then proposes a rejection of the concept of historical time in favor of the presumably timeless universality of myth. Yet as some literary theories suggest and as an examination of Caribbean fiction substantiates, myth and history are not mutually exclusive modes of literary expression— myth relegated to the realm of ahistorical transcendence and history to the "prison" of documentary realism.

3

The historical reality that all writers of the Caribbean must come to terms with is the cultural dislocation and fragmentation brought about by the European conquest of the Americas. Accordingly, the West Indian writer has all too often been paralyzed by a vision of the Caribbean as the site of historical and cultural shipwreck. Until very recently, writers of the West Indies overlooked the fact that the historic clash of cultures in the New World signaled not only the loss of a cultural heritage, but also the beginning of a new one. The Caribbean was the gateway to the New World, and its history, as Roberto González Echevarría points out, is "one of beginnings or foundations. . . . Colonialism, slavery, racial mixture and strife, and consequently revolution and independence movements all occurred first in the Caribbean."[1]

In contrast to V. S. Naipaul's vision of a barren, uncreative West Indian past, novelists such as Alejo Carpentier, Edouard Glissant, and Wilson Harris recognize a capacity for creation and renewal in the myths, legends, and folktales that arose from the encounter of Amerindian, African, and European cultures in the Americas. For these writers, the folk or mythic imagination is the key to artistic vision and historical understanding. They view the folk traditions and history of the Americas as the source of a new form of fictional discourse in which they attempt to reshape traditional literary values associated with the colonial past, while at the same time proposing an alternative to "fossilized," static conceptions of New World history. In their novels and essays, all three writers have addressed the relationship between the historical origins of Caribbean or New World culture and the problems of literary expression.

The interaction of myth and history therefore plays a fundamental role in their attempts to redefine the aesthetics of the novel in the context of New World culture. Wilson Harris, for example, proposes a revolution in the novel based on a philosophy of history that takes into account the "subconscious imagination" of the folk traditions of the West Indian people: "a drama of consciousness which reads back through the shock of place and time for omens of capacity that were latent, unrealized, within the clash of cultures and movements of peoples into the South Americas and West Indies."[2] Alejo Carpentier and Edouard Glissant suggest a similar relationship, and even ques-

4

tion whether there is any meaningful difference between the novelist and the historian. In their fiction, the "drama of consciousness" is the creative exploration of a violent history of rupture, conflict, and new beginnings.

Their notion of a "poetics" of history is akin to the Vichian concept of the interrelationship of myth, language, and history. When Glissant says that Caribbean writers should reinvent their history by a process of "poetic divination," he recalls Vico's concept of myth as both a form of historical knowledge and a method of historical inquiry (*sapienza poetica*). For Vico, myth is a way of thinking—the speculative, analogical thinking of the creative imagination.[3] More recently, from the perspective of modern structural anthropology, Lévi-Strauss uses the term *bricolage* to describe the concrete, metaphorical thought processes at work in myth.[4]

Given the historical rupture with the ancestral past (whether Amerindian, African, East Indian, or Chinese) experienced by the majority of the peoples of the Caribbean, the status of myth is necessarily a problematic one for Caribbean writers. The concept of myth itself is notoriously complex and its use across disciplines is often contradictory. The original definition of myth is narration or story. Myths are usually considered the spontaneous expression of a people, associated with religious beliefs and ritual; thus, Mircea Eliade's definition of myths as "sacred stories." Isidore Okpewho, however, rejects the dichotomy between sacred and secular used to distinguish myths from other popular traditions, such as fables, folktales, and legends; he emphasizes the oral and inventive aspects of these communal narratives.[5] Similarly, G. S. Kirk challenges the notions of myth that have developed over the last century and emphasizes the speculative, imaginative content of myth. This type of orally transmitted narrative speculates on the unknown or some as-yet unresolved problem of a community.[6]

In regard to the problem-reflecting aspect of myth, Daniel-Henri Pageaux points to the interrelationship of myth, history and story:

> Myth is History and not just story. It is the History of a group, a community, a cultural collectivity. It is fostered by the History of the group. . . . but it is always a reinterpretation of History. As such, myth

5

always augments, because historically it only appears as compensatory History. The absence (real or perceived as such) of certain historical realities or factors explains how myth emerges, is told and is written as second History. This definition . . . permits us to see mythic (Hi)story as a compensatory factor in a situation perceived as frustrating, in a situation of suffering and absence.[7]

The novels of Carpentier, Harris, and Glissant assume the role of myth as historical memory and speculative inquiry intended to provoke consciousness. For Carpentier and Harris, myth is the tradition of creativity common to all peoples. As part of their strategy for inscribing Caribbean culture in the universal lexicon, they combine mythic symbols from various African, Amerindian, and European traditions in their novels. Glissant, however, questions all universalizing theories of history and culture. Like Fanon, he rejects the "poetics of oneness" implicit in the archetype, emphasizing instead the specificity and difference of West Indian cultural expression.[8]

In his general discussion of myth, Glissant notes that the link between history and literature is first expressed in myth; history appears in myth as the beginnings of historical perception (intuition or *pressentiment du passé*), and literature as the impulse toward creative invention ("memories of the future"). In this sense, myth is capable of both preserving and producing history through memory and the transformation of consciousness.[9] This description of myth is similar to Glissant's own concept of the novel as the "prophetic vision of the past," but one in which the unconscious is made conscious.

Glissant then contrasts the creole folktale with the historical development of myth in the West, which leads to the dynastic principle of genealogical filiation, the claim of sacred origins and linear succession for the purpose of legitimizing power and control. He goes on to say that in the Western tradition "myth consecrates the word and thus dedicates it to the ritual of writing by anticipating it"; the creole folktale, however, with its wily strategies of survival and resistance, "proceeds by sacrilegious attack. What it attacks is above all the sacredness of the written sign. The Caribbean folktale is the beacon of a history carried off course by edict and by law. It is anti-edict and anti-law, that is to say anti-writing."[10] As such, the creole folktale is a disruptive counterpoetics, which undermines transcendental notions of literature and history.

Although Carpentier and Harris differ from Glissant in their approach to myth as cultural archetype, strategies of disruption play an increasingly important role in their later fiction. All three writers challenge the imposed unity of dominant cultures and attempt to redefine Western universality in terms of a global perspective based on an understanding of the "necessity for complex mutuality between cultures," or as Glissant says, the poetics of "difference by mutual consent." Caribbean writers are therefore involved in a dual process of naming and unnaming; the first by laying claim to their own past and their own traditions, and the latter by dismantling the hidden mechanisms of political and cultural domination.[11]

The literary project of Glissant, like that of Carpentier and Harris, is to reveal the hidden traces of historical experience erased from the collective memory of an exploited and oppressed people, so that history may be reconceived as a future history to be made, *l'histoire à faire*.[12] Of these three writers, Harris is the least inclined to pose this problem as a conflict between the West and those cultures excluded from the Hegelian grand narrative of history; his aim is to expose all "*partial* orders masquerading as totalities or absolutes."[13] Although popular traditions (myths, legends, folktales) figure prominently in the theoretical formulation of the literary projects of these writers, there are important differences in their ideological perspectives on the nature of social and cultural transformation in the historical process. Nevertheless, the history of cultural and psychic dismemberment, the reconstruction of historical memory, and a future-oriented vision of possibility characterize the shared discourse of Carpentier, Harris, and Glissant on the history and culture of the Caribbean.

The Cuban writer Alejo Carpentier (1904–1980) is considered the first novelist to incorporate the Caribbean region as a whole in his fiction, drawing the lines of historical and cultural convergence among the islands of the Caribbean archipelago in novels such as *El reino de este mundo* and *El siglo de las luces*. In each of these novels, the Caribbean is the site of a revolutionary social transformation that has hemispheric, indeed global impact. It was in the prologue to his novel about the Haitian Revolution, *El reino de este mundo*, that Carpentier

7

introduced his notion of "marvelous realism," the literary concept that would influence a later generation of writers in Latin America as well as the Caribbean.

Undoubtedly, the most influential aspect of Carpentier's concept of marvelous realism is its emphasis on the creative potential of Caribbean and Latin American history and culture. An underlying factor, however, in Carpentier's formulation of this concept is the need to resolve a set of difficult if not conflicting demands—the desire to reinsert himself into a New World cultural context after living in Europe for more than a decade, the desire to go beyond traditional realism and to use the innovative experiments of modernism, while at the same time incorporating the distinctive features of the landscape, history, and popular traditions of the Americas in his fiction.

In an essay on the problem of literary form, Gordon Rohlehr points out the tension between the attraction to popular oral traditions and the aesthetics of modernism in the literature of many Anglophone Caribbean writers:

> If the oral tradition directs our attention to assemblies of people, the lime, the calypso tent, church, grounation, cult, drum, dance, performance, narrative, song, and sermon, modernist aesthetics highlights the separateness or the alienation of the individual, who is placed or lost in a universe of open possibilities, where he must create self, style and form. Modernist aesthetics may raise problems of void or vortex, chaos or silence, the irrelevance of the individual, the dehumanization of art and the emergence in an incomprehensible universe of the art object as its own circular self-contained world, exploring itself, echoing itself, and sometimes with enviable, worm-like flexibility, even copulating itself.[14]

According to Glissant, this tension is a result of the abrupt transition between orality and writing in most Third World cultures. He considers the "irruption into modernity," as opposed to the gradual development of literary traditions in the West, to be one of the common elements of the fiction of colonial and postcolonial societies. Glissant describes his own approach as one of constructing his fiction on the boundaries of orality and written discourse.[15] Even Harris, possibly the most hermetic modernist among these three writers, claims the limbo dancer and vodun ceremony as folk paradigms of the "arts of the imagination."[16]

In their experiments with literary form, Carpentier, Harris, and Glissant use folk traditions such as the maroon legends, the myth of El Dorado, and carnival as a means of exploring problems of cultural identity, historical presence, and writing. Although these three writers are very much involved in modernist and, especially in the case of Glissant, postmodernist debates about origins, identity, and presence, the void in their novels is more than just a linguistic or ontological abstraction. It is above all the historically determined rupture of domination and dispossession in the Caribbean. In their representations of Caribbean history, these writers attempt to bridge the gap between experience and meaning by a creative transformation of consciousness.

PART ONE

Myth as a
Historical Mode:
Lo real maravilloso
americano

CHAPTER 1

Lo real maravilloso
in Caribbean Fiction

Alejo Carpentier's concept of *lo real maravilloso* has its counterpart in both the French and English literature of the Caribbean. The notion of a "marvelous American reality" is the culmination of a cultural reorientation and renovation of the arts that began in the early decades of the twentieth century with such literary movements as surrealism, negritude, and indigenism. *Lo real maravilloso*, with its emphasis on the mythohistorical heritage of the Americas, represents the beginning of a dialogue among several writers of the Caribbean who were concerned with establishing a New World cultural identity based on the shared heritage of all of its peoples.

In 1956 at the first international Congress of Black Artists and Writers, the Haitian novelist Jacques Stéphen Alexis spoke of *le réalisme merveilleux* as the characteristic mode of Haitian artistic expression:

> Haitian art in effect presents the real with its retinue of the strange, the
> fantastic, the dream, half-light, mystery, and the marvelous. . . . our

art tends toward the most exact sensuous representation of reality, toward creative intuition, toward distinctive style, and expressive power. This art does not hesitate before deformity, the shocking, violent contrast, before antithesis as a means of expressing emotion and aesthetic investigation . . . it achieves a new more contrasting harmony, a composition harmonious in its contradiction, with a wholly inner grace, born of the unusual and the antithetical.[1]

For Alexis, the marvelous in Haitian art is a dynamic, all-embracing realism linked to myth, symbol, and even the sacred, that goes beyond preestablished notions of harmony, beauty, and logic. Yet it is firmly rooted in the everyday realities of the Haitian people, since at the center of its violent profusion of contradictory forms "man bursts forth, working toward his destiny and happiness."[2]

Marvelous realism, according to Alexis, is above all a realism rooted in reality in that its source is the expressive language of the Haitian people—their folktales, legends, music, dance, religious beliefs—and its focus is the drama of human conflict in all its manifestations: "What is the Marvelous then if not the imagery in which a people envelop their experience, reflect their conception of the world. . . . The Marvelous includes to be sure naïveté, mystification if not mysticism, but it has been shown that it may also include something else. . . . Isn't it also the cosmic dream of abundance and fraternity of those people who still suffer from hunger and want?"[3]

The intellectual and literary context of Alexis's discussion of Haitian art and marvelous realism is the redefinition of culture as a truly universal humanism that recognizes the aspirations and contributions of all peoples. The definition of culture thus becomes more than just an inventory of literary or artistic works; it emphasizes the human basis of all cultural activity: "Culture is a fundamental concept that embraces the whole life of a people, from its beginnings, through its gradual development, up to its modern organization: culture is a ceaseless becoming whose origins are lost in the night of time and whose perspectives are blurred in the mist of the future." Equally important is the recognition of the collective origins of all forms of cultural expression, including the literary creations of individual writers. For while writers may transform the collective consciousness of their society, they are also conditioned by it. This dialectical

14

relationship between the writer and the national culture underlies Alexis's conception of marvelous realism.[4]

Nevertheless, while individual artists may consciously or unconsciously incorporate elements of the national traditions in their works, Alexis maintains that the truly avant-garde artists in Haiti must transcend the irrational, mystical, and animistic elements of their national heritage by rejecting those aspects of it that obscure the dynamic realism at its core. It is thus a matter of uncovering the most vital elements of those cultural traditions, or as Alexis puts it "to set back on its feet that which too often walks on its head."[5] Alexis's marvelous realism is a visionary art in that the fusion of the real and the marvelous offers the possibility of transforming human consciousness. The literary critic Michael Dash cites a later essay in which Alexis writes: "The mythical and the marvelous can, when understood in a rational way, become powerful levers for providing men with a vision, for creating a realistic art and literature, for transforming the world."[6]

A related topic in Alexis's 1956 speech was his discussion of the debate over formalism and realism, which has been a persistent concern of modern writers. This topic was of particular concern to the black writers who participated in the congress since one of the principal aims of the congress was to establish the nature and future direction of black literary expression. In his essentially Marxist analysis, Alexis strongly denounced the tendency toward "pure art" as the cultural expression of an artistic fringe that places more importance on unbridled artistic freedom than on human freedom. He maintains that throughout the history of culture, there has been a pendular movement between the two poles of realism and formalism, depending on whether the ruling classes were in a dynamic or decadent phase, but that the most enduring creations of all great artists have been linked to realism and the humanism of their times. For Alexis, realism is concerned with human achievements, capabilities, and interests as opposed to the abstractions of formalist literature. As an example of this, he criticizes the surrealist experiments as "cold, analytical games" detached from human struggles and hopes.[7]

Although Alexis denounces formalist anarchy, he does not reject experimentation with form as long as human concerns govern its artistic purpose. Nor is he interested in a cold, analytical realism; he calls for a living realism "tied to the magic of the universe," a realism that would include the naive, the lyrical, the mystical, and the naturalistic. The integration of all of these elements constitutes Alexis's definition of marvelous realism. He maintains, however, that Haitian art is fundamentally linked to life: "Yes, we are dreamers, but infinitely realistic."[8]

Alexis also addresses the issue of negritude, which was a focus of intense debate at the congress. He points out that in the assimilationist thinking of the Haitian upper class, Haiti was merely a "cultural province" of France and that this attitude had provoked an extremely nationalist response on the part of many Haitian writers and artists, particularly those advocates of negritude. Although Alexis admits that the negritude movement generally had a positive impact on Haitian culture, he warns against its excessive populist and Africanist orientation, which he felt obscured the cultural autonomy of the Haitian people. While he supports solidarity with Africa and recognizes the dominant contribution of Africa to Haitian culture, Alexis emphasizes Haiti's New World cultural identity as the synthesis of Taino, African, and European cultural roots.

Michael Dash interprets Alexis's 1956 speech and later writings as a reaction against what he considers the negative assumptions of negritude: the perception of the colonial past as sterile and uncreative, the alienated sense of a lost African heritage, and the notion of a homogeneous black culture.[9] It seems to me, however, that Alexis was primarily concerned with placing the discussion of Haitian culture in the context of the Americas; that is, asserting its New World identity over its Old World links (though he never rejects the cultural contributions of either Africa or Europe). Alexis continually stresses the cultural affinities between Haiti and the other areas of the Caribbean and Latin America. In addition to the cultural and social similarities, he points to the historical relationship that links Haiti to the other people of the Americas: "The way they have helped each other win their respective independence struggles, the support Dessalines and Pétion gave to the Mexican general Mina, to Miranda, to Bolivar, the Haitian volunteers who spilled their blood on Latin American soil, all this created a fraternity which favors the confluence of cultures."[10]

Alexis's Carribean/New World perspective is a continuation of the ideas of his mentor Jacques Roumain, who also promoted an understanding of the common cultural and historical legacy of the peoples of the Caribbean and Latin America.[11] Like Roumain, Alexis was a political activist who came into conflict with the Haitian government. He is believed to have been killed by Duvalier's Tonton Macoutes in 1961. Michael Dash evaluates Alexis's literary contribution as follows: "To Alexis this new conception of realism [*réalisme merveilleux*] signified a way of reaching beyond conventional realism to explore the spiritual world of the folk and establish the continuity that integrated all the various elements of Haitian history. . . . His attitude to historical reality had the potential for changing in an unprecedented way the ideological positions and creative imagination of Haiti."[12]

Although Alexis never mentions Carpentier in his discussions of marvelous realism, he was undoubtedly familiar with the Cuban writer's use of the term. Aside from the nearly identical terminology, Alexis's emphasis on the primacy of the concrete historical reality of Haiti as a source of the "marvelous," his emphasis on the heterogeneity of Haitian culture, as well as his experiments with Haitian folk culture, suggest a close link to Carpentier's concept of *lo real maravilloso*.[13]

For Carpentier, Haiti represented the "magical crossroads" of New World history and culture. The "magic" of Haiti is identified with vodun, the spiritual beliefs of a people who, as George Lamming once wrote, "have retained a racial, and historic, desire to worship their original gods."[14] In Caribbean discourse, Haiti is often portrayed as the site of a revelation of consciousness. This is true in Aimé Césaire's evocation of Toussaint L'Ouverture and the vodun ritual in *Cahier d'un retour au pays natal* (originally published in 1939), in Lamming's own use of the Ceremony of the Souls in San Cristobal, Haiti's fictional counterpart in the *Season of Adventure* (1960) and *Water with Berries* (1971), and even in C. L. R. James's epic account of the Haitian Revolution in *Black Jacobins* (1938). Just as Césaire claimed Haiti as the place "where Negritude stood up for the first time and swore by its humanity," Carpentier in the 1940s saw Haiti as the antithesis and antidote to European cultural domination. Although he was of European ancestry, Afro-Caribbean religious practices held a central place in Carpentier's first novel *Ecue-Yamba-O* (1933); and despite his repudiation of this early work, he would repeatedly return to the African presence in Caribbean history and culture in later novels, such as *El reino de este mundo, El siglo de las luces,* and *Concierto barroco.*

After leaving Cuba for political reasons, Carpentier spent over a decade in Paris (1928–1939) where he collaborated with the surrealists. During the heady literary and political disputes of this period, he sided with his close friend Robert Desnos and the other dissidents expelled from André Breton's group.[15] On the eve of World War II, disillusioned with Europe and his experience with the surrealist avantgarde, Carpentier returned to the Americas and formulated his own concept of the marvelous, which appeared in the prologue to *El reino* (1949).

He explains that it was during a trip to Haiti in 1943 that he recognized the true source of the marvelous, *lo real maravilloso,* in the landscape, myths, and history of the Americas: "After feeling the genuine sorcery of the landscape of Haiti, discovering magic omens along the red roads of the Central Plateau, hearing the Petro and Rada drums, I found myself comparing the marvelous reality I had just experienced with the tiresome pretense of provoking the marvelous that characterized certain literature of the last thirty years." Carpentier goes on to say that he came to realize that the marvelous reality, *lo real maravilloso,* he first experienced in Haiti is the legacy of all of the Americas:

> It is found at every step in the lives of men for whom dates are recorded in the history of the Continent. . . . from the seekers of the Fountain of Eternal Youth and the Golden City of Manoa, to certain rebels of the first hour or certain modern heroes of our wars of independence. . . .
> And the fact is that, because of its virgin landscape, its formation, its ontology; because of the Revelation its recent discovery constituted, the fertile crossbreedings it produced, America is far from having exhausted its wealth of mythologies.[16]

The aesthetic principle that underlies the concept of marvelous realism in both Carpentier and Alexis is the notion of "harmonious contradiction."[17] What Carpentier does in his formulation of *lo real maravilloso* is achieve an apparent inversion of the surrealist *merveilleux,* which was based on the juxtaposition of disparate realities derived from the subconscious. By using a term that in itself seems contradictory—the union of the real and the marvelous—Carpentier intended to undermine the validity of the surrealist approach while at the same time suggesting that the marvelous lay elsewhere; that is, in the conflicting realities of New World history and culture.[18]

Carpentier views the discovery of the Americas as a revelation, an unprecedented event that changed the course of universal history. As a result of this historic encounter of the Old World and the New, for the first time humankind gains a full sense of the world in which they live. Not only does the discovery enlarge the dimension of human interaction in a global sense, but also it brings about the mixed racial and ethnic heritage that would constitute the distinctive character of New World culture.[19] Comparing this phenomenon to a similar cultural process that took place in the Mediterannean, the protagonist of Carpentier's *Los pasos perdidos,* for example, observes that in the Americas there "had not been the amalgam of related peoples, such as history had fused at certain crossroads of Ulysses' sea, but of the great races of the world, the most widely separated, the most divergent, those which for centuries had ignored the fact that they inhabited the same planet."[20]

Carpentier considers the mixed racial and ethnic heritage of the Americas as the manifestation of the creative potential of New World art. The historical fact of cultural *mestizaje* thus becomes the central metaphor in the aesthetics of "symbiosis, amalgamation, and transformation" proposed in his concept of *lo real maravilloso.* Having established the synthesis of heterogeneous elements as the basic characteristic of marvelous realism, Carpentier refers to the narrative style that corresponds to the complex realities of the Americas as a form of New World *baroque.* The use of this term suggests an exuberant, stylistic duality similar to Jacques Stéphen Alexis's description of Haitian art. Furthermore, Carpentier points out that New World baroque is not the imitation of any other art form because it challenges the notions of good and bad art inherent in all existing styles. It establishes a different scale of values by bringing together a new arrangement of elements, textures, juxtapositions, convolutions of form, and metaphor.[21]

According to Carpentier the task of Latin American or New World writers is to bring the distinctive features of their reality into the realm of universal culture by naming everything: "everything that defines, involves, and surrounds us: everything that functions with the force of *context*—to situate it in the universal. . . . Our ceiba, our trees, adorned with flowers or not, must be made universal by means of precisely chosen words." The necessity of naming things results in a narrative language—a baroque prose—that attempts to capture the density and proportions of New World realities. Carpentier maintains that baroque is the legitimate style of New World art: "Our art was always baroque: from the magnificent pre-Columbian sculpture and codices to the best contemporary [Latin] American fiction, down to the colonial cathedrals and monasteries of our continent. . . . Let's not fear, then, baroque style, in our representation of contexts, in our vision of the human being entangled in the word."[22]

Carpentier's classification of New World art as essentially baroque is based on the premise that the bold use of metaphor characteristic of baroque style finds its parallel in the language of myth. For as Wylie Sypher observes in his study of the interrelations of art and literature, "The language of myth is, prevailingly, metaphor, since metaphor dramatizes the world, anthropomorphizes reality."[23] Metaphor, the concrete logic of myth, functions in baroque imagery as a means of organizing differences and contrasts so that "every difference is resemblance by surprise."[24]

In Carpentier's thinking the new, the strange, and the unfamiliar in New World landscapes and social realities—the marvelous—must be inscribed in the universal lexicon, even if its universality can only be established by means of contrast and difference. Thus the aesthetics of oppositions that he proposes—or *antithesis*, to use Alexis's term—often leads to a reversal of the familiar combinations of terms, a new scale of values.[25]

Consequently, the contrasts between European and New World culture play a significant role in Carpentier's formulation of the

20

concept of *lo real maravilloso*. Europe always serves as the primary reference or counterpoint in his attempt to identify the distinctive character of New World reality. Commenting on Carpentier's attitude toward European culture, the Martinican poet and novelist Edouard Glissant observes that if Carpentier judges the West harshly, it is because of an overbearing necessity to confront the differences between these two worlds: "the West, stripped of the taboos with which it has adorned itself in order to perpetuate its domination; [and] a new world, with its excesses, its aspirations, its own values. . . . But at the same time [his] work addresses an experience common to millions of people; since the debate is about a clash of cultures, and what is at stake here is a possible avenue toward unity."[26] As the Martinican poet recognizes, Carpentier does not reject European culture but seeks a redefinition of universal culture that would make it possible to assert the value of his own culture and focus his literary efforts where he deemed they would be most fruitful—in the Americas.

Carpentier's formulation of the concept of marvelous realism therefore involved an ideological as well as an aesthetic project. In his essay on the search for Caribbean cultural identity, James Irish rightly considers *lo real maravilloso* a further development of *mundonovismo,* the movement of New World consciousness that originated in Latin America in the aftermath of the nineteenth-century independence struggles.[27] Irlemar Chiampi, however, traces the ideology of New World consciousness to the moment of its discovery and the period of the conquest. Furthermore, she maintains that the persistent recurrence of the notion of the marvelous in discussions of American reality among Latin American intellectuals has always been in response to moments of historical crisis: the discovery, conquest and colonization, independence struggles, and postindependence period. From the 1920s to the 1940s the major focus of *mundonovismo* was the notion of cultural *mestizaje*, which was a reflection of desire to reject European and North American political and cultural hegemony. Chiampi discusses the idea of cultural *mestizaje* in the writings of José Vasconcelos, Ricardo Rojas, Uslar Pietri, Lezama Lima, and Alejo Carpentier. It is in the latter's concept of *lo real maravilloso*, however, that she sees the convergence of ideology and form based on a principle of "non-disjunction" (both in terms of the notion of cultural synthesis as well as the fusion of myth and history), which characterizes the contemporary Latin American narrative.[28]

Neither *mundonovismo* nor its literary corollary, marvelous realism, would have any significant impact on the Caribbean as a whole, however, until the issues of racial and colonial subjugation were challenged head-on. That challenge came in the form of the black consciousness movements of the 1920s and 1930s, and was expressed in the works of writers as diverse as Nicolás Guillén, Aimé Césaire, Alejo Carpentier, and Jacques Roumain. This period represented the first phase in a process of cultural decolonization that would make possible the identification of the peoples of the Caribbean in the context of the Americas. And subsequently, it is the acceptance of the cultural plurality of the Americas that has led such novelists as Jacques Stéphen Alexis, Edouard Glissant, and Wilson Harris to uphold literary views similar to those proposed by Alejo Carpentier in his concept of marvelous realism.

In his formulation of the concept of *lo real maravilloso americano*, Carpentier considered cultural *mestizaje* an indication of the creative potential of New World patterns of syncretism. Rather than viewing this amalgam as bizarre, deformed, or incongruous (the negative connotation of the baroque), he recognized in this "impossible harmony" the positive roots of a new cultural synthesis. Similarly, Glissant and Harris see in the contrasting elements of New World culture a capacity for overcoming what is generally perceived as a fragmented, divided consciousness. The desire to "see those fragments whole" informs both Glissant's *poétique de la relation* and Harris's poetics of the "cross-cultural imagination."[29]

The process of creolization (*métissage/mestizaje*) is the cultural model for Glissant's *poétique de la relation*, the dynamics of identity and difference in the complex interrelationship of cultures. Like Carpentier, Glissant chooses Montaigne over Hegel and rejects the nonrelational absolutes of Western cultural discourse. In *Le discours antillais,* he notes the shift in contemporary culture from a notion of sameness that erases difference and renders the Other invisible toward a concept of cultural diversity that not only acknowledges the right to difference, *le droit à la différence,* but also the right to pres-

22

ence, "to name oneself in the world."[30] The work of the writer is then one of cultural *insertion* within a global framework, based on the principle of diversity (*le divers*) rather than sameness (*le même*), transversality rather than universality.

Some studies of marvelous realism as defined by Carpentier have described this concept as the literary expression of underdevelopment.[31] In an essay on "The Novel of the Americas," Edouard Glissant discusses two important aspects of the literary discourse of Latin American and Caribbean writers related to the historical fact of colonialism and underdevelopment: the "irruption into modernity" and the "tormented link between writing and orality." The violence of the conquest and the distortions of colonialism and slavery result in an "open, splintered, unaligned" sense of time and space. Glissant points out that the literatures of these cultures have not had a gradual, continuous development such as that of Europe, which evolved "from the collective lyricism of Homer to the harsh dissections of Beckett. They have had to take on everything all at once."[32] As expressions of different historical and social realities, these literatures do not fit comfortably into either the framework of traditional realism or the accepted notions of modernism.

Many of the characteristics that Carpentier identifies with the baroque, Glissant associates with orality. The tension between orality and writing, implicit in Carpentier's concept of marvelous realism, is brought to the forefront of the problematics of literary expression in Glissant's poetics. For Glissant, the creole languages of the Caribbean are the embodiment of disparate cultural dimensions brought together by force during the period of plantation slavery. As such they are languages of constraint and *unconscious* refusal, engaged in a struggle to overcome silence, *le non-dit,* and censure, *l'édit.* Creole orality breaks up the linear logic of syntax with its indirect, elliptical style marked by heavy rhythmic repetitions, syllabic blurrings, inversions, and hidden meanings. In his own work Glissant aims to *synthesize* orality and writing—"written syntax and rhythmic speech, the 'acquired' practices of writing and the oral 'reflex', the solitude of writing and participation in a common song."[33]

For the Guyanese novelist Wilson Harris, Caribbean folk traditions are manifestations of a capacity for creativity as well as intuitive strategies for dealing with historical crises. Where Glissant emphasizes the *détour* (strategies of evasion and resistance) in creole language and folktales, Harris points to the transformative power of the folk imagination in such "arts of the dispossessed" as West Indian limbo and Haitian vodun. In the essay "History, Fable and Myth," Harris notes that the limbo dance of West Indian carnival celebrations is said to have originated on the crowded slave ships of the Middle Passage. Citing the connection between the limbo dancer's spiderlike transformation and the Caribbean Anancy fables in Edward Brathwaite's "Islands," Harris interprets the emergence of limbo as the slaves' subconscious means of "bridging the gap between an outer frame and an inner dislocation"; that is, the symbolic transcendence of the condition of confinement in the transition from the African past to the New World in the Americas.[34]

According to Harris, the limbo dance represents "a profound art of compensation which seeks to re-play a dismemberment of tribes . . . and to invoke at the same time a curious psychic re-assembly of the parts of the dead god or gods. And that re-assembly . . . issued from a state of cramp to articulate a new growth." Haitian vodun, with its syncretic fusions of African and European religious practices, is similar to the limbo phenomenon in that "it breaks the tribal monolith of the past and re-assembles an inter-tribal or cross-cultural community of families."[35] Limbo and vodun are thus viewed as creative responses to the traumas of history, and as such—according to Harris—should serve as cultural models for a new approach to the history of the Americas.

Harris maintains that conventional history (regardless of its ideological perspective) tends to erect a "monolithic wall" in which the Caribbean is conceived only in terms of an endless cycle of imperialist aggression, whereas the limbo and vodun phenomena reveal "original dislocations in the pattern of exploiter/exploited charted by the historian."[36] These dislocations are primarily psychic transformations; accordingly, Harris's novels are fables of rebirth that point toward the "dawn of new consciousness" in the aftermath of historical conflict.

What interests Harris most about vodun and limbo is the "spatial logic" of their dance forms. He compares the obliteration of the boundaries between interior and exterior space that is expressed by the vodun dancer's movement in the possession trance and the limbo dancer's "spider metamorphosis" to the dynamics of literary creation. As in his own fiction, time and consciousness are represented through the "protean reality of space."[37] In the "Guiana Quartet," for example, narrative is conceived as a *reconstruction* of consciousness in which time is experienced as "primordial memory" or inner subjective time. Since he rejects the concept of history as linear chronology, time in Harris's novels is shattered and reassembled so that past, present, and future are presented in a variety of discontinuous patterns.

The "womb of space," as Harris's interpretation of limbo and vodun suggests, is his metaphor for the transformative capacity of the human imagination. The psychic and cultural void produced by historical rupture is reconceived as the fertile space of regeneration— the "untamed potential of re-birth."[38] It is in this space that a new sense of community, no longer based solely on the principle of *filiation,* is envisioned as a bridge across cultures. Rather than the symmetrical, transparent totalities that have for so long dominated cultural and literary discourse, Harris (like Carpentier and Glissant) proposes the asymmetrical, complex interrelations of the cross-cultural imagination.

For Harris as well as Carpentier and Glissant, the Caribbean is the geographic and cultural space where narratives of identity and difference reveal the need (and the potential) for this new vision of community. These writers have created a fictional discourse aimed at breaking through the cultural barriers of colonialism and its hierarchical notions of identity and historical reality. In their innovative explorations of space, time, and language, all three writers redefine the relationship between the folk imagination and writing, myth and history. For them, writing in the marginalized space of colonial and postcolonial societies is a creative act of repossession.

CHAPTER 2

The Folk Imagination and History:
El reino de este mundo,
The Secret Ladder,
and *Le quatrième siècle*

$\mathbf{I}$n their novels, Carpentier, Harris, and Glissant challenge conventional notions of history and the fictional representation of history. The legendary maroon serves as a medium for historical inquiry and exploration of novelistic form in *El reino de este mundo* (1949), *The Secret Ladder* (1963), and *Le quatrième siècle* (1964). The main focus of these novels is the nature of historical change in the struggle for freedom. They question whether history is a "circumstantial riddle"—a meaningless cycle of oppression and rebellion—or a process of continuity, conflict, and transformation. The folk imagination functions as a revolutionary, transformative element in the formal structures of the three texts, but myth—the myths of the African past as well as the European notion of material progress—is subject to the manipulations of power.

Alejo Carpentier wrote *El reino de este mundo* with its now famous prologue during a period of resurgence in the *mundonovismo* movement. Roberto González Echevarría describes the Carpentier of the 1940s as an American Ulysses in search of "that elusive Golden Age

27

when fable and history were one."[1] The historical context of *El reino* is the period of the Haitian slave revolt in the last half of the eighteenth century, which culminated in the establishment of the first black republic in the Americas at the beginning of the nineteenth century.

The historical focus of *El reino* is not, however, history told from the point of view of great men; some of the most important historical figures are glaringly absent. Instead, Carpentier recreates the events of that history as experienced by the ordinary slave. Ti Noel, a groom on the Lenormand de Mezy sugarcane plantation, is the protagonist who witnesses the historical episodes that shake the island of Saint Domingue at the end of the eighteenth century. Through the consciousness of Ti Noel, Carpentier merges the mythic and historical cycles of the novel. Thus the folk imagination (the oral traditions and religious beliefs of the Haitian slaves) is the vehicle for the author's experiments with space and time in the narrative.

The mythic or folk imagination may play either a conservative or revolutionary role in historical consciousness. In *El reino de este mundo*, Carpentier emphasizes the revolutionary, transformative potential of myth.[2] The first half of the novel deals with the time of the Great Pacts, the period of the legendary Mackandal and Bouckman. Mackandal, the least historically documented of the two folk heroes, is an African priest, visionary, and rebel who passes down the oral traditions of the African past to the New World slaves. Revered as a great storyteller, he conveys a living sense of that past: "He spoke of the great migrations of tribes, of age-long wars, of epic battles in which the animals had been allies of men. He knew the story of Adonhueso, of the King of Angola, of King Da, the incarnation of the Serpent, which is the eternal beginning, never ending, who took his pleasure mystically with a queen who was the Rainbow, patroness of the Waters and of all Bringing Forth."[3] Mackandal's stories about the serpent-god Damballah, "mystical representation of the eternal wheel" and African symbol of cosmic unity, are central to Carpentier's concept of time in this early novel as a combination of the cyclical patterns of nature and historical continuum. Myth is not, however, presented in *El reino* as a timeless universal untouched by historical conflict.

Although the mythic imagination with its fusions of time and space in which everything is possible (the marvelous in the surrealist sense) is the model for Carpentier's experiments with time and space in this novel, his use of the culture myths of the African slaves also serves another function. Mackandal's stories of Africa are intended to negate the idea of a cultural void as the necessary legacy of slavery—a prevalent theme in discussions of Caribbean history and culture. These stories are more than nostalgic evocations of the glories of the African past since through them Mackandal perpetuates historical memory and the quest for freedom.

In *El reino* Mackandal is the storyteller who preserves a "tradition of freedom" and the wounded hero whose mutilation results in the promise of deliverance. The loss of an arm in an accident at the sugarcane mill leads to his discovery of a means for bringing about the liberation of his people. No longer capable of heavy work at the mill, he is assigned a new task as shepherd. During his long hours in the pastures of the Lenormand de Mezy estate, he finds the poison mushrooms and other wild plants that he will use to carry out a "crusade of extermination" against the slave owners.

Since his injury made him unsuitable for any important work, Mackandal's escape from the plantation into the mountains is hardly noticed. Furthermore, it was commonly understood that any African of Mandingue origin "was a potential fugitive [maroon]. Mandingue was a synonym for intractable, rebellious, a devil" (27). Mackandal lives up to that reputation when with the collaboration of trustworthy disciples he commences his campaign of poison, which like an invisible plague kills animals and people by the hundreds:

> The sinister hammering of coffins could be heard at all hours. . . . In the shadow of the silver crucifixes that moved up and down the roads, green poison, yellow poison, or poison that had no color went creeping along, coming down the kitchen chimneys, slipping through the cracks of locked doors, like some irrepressible creeper seeking the shade to turn bodies to shades. From *Miserere* to *De Profundis* the voices of the subchanters went on, hour after hour, in a sinister antiphony. (34–35)

It is only after Mackandal is betrayed by a fellow slave that the slave masters discover the source of the campaign of terror. According to historical records, Mackandal began his insurrection against the creole plantocracy in 1751, but it took them seven years to capture the rebel slave.[4] In Carpentier's fictional account of Mackandal's revolt, he emphasizes the slave owners' helplessness in the face of what the slaves believe to be the maroon's supernatural powers. When all else fails to put an end to the "march of poison," they resort to their own necromancers and healers, revealing how thin a line separated the "enlightened" European from the African slaves who were described as "Philistines, adoring Dagon in the Ark" (78).

The colonists console themselves with tales of their grandfathers who, like the pirates L'Esnambuc, Bertrand D'Ogeron, and Du Rausset, "had founded the colony of their own initiative making their will law, without ever being intimidated by edicts issued in Paris or the gentle reprimands of the *Code Noir*" (40). But the slaves continue their dreams of insurrection and freedom as they await the "call of the great conch shells" that would announce the return of Mackandal: "One day he would give the sign for the great uprising and the Lords of Back There, headed by Damballah, the Master of the Roads, and Ogoun Master of the Swords, would bring the thunder and lightning and unleash the cyclone that would round out the work of men's hands" (42).

In the mythic imagination of his people, Mackandal's spirit reigns everywhere. They believe in his power of metamorphosis; like Proteus he has the capacity to transform himself into any animal, bird, or insect. Before his capture and execution, he appears in human form for the last time at a vodun ceremony during the Christmas season: "Behind the Mother Drum rose the human figure of Macandal. The Mandingue Macandal, the man Macandal. The One-Armed. The Restored. . . . Something of his sojourns in mysterious places seemed to cling to him, something of his successive attires of scales, bristles, fur. His chin had taken on a feline sharpness, and his eyes seemed to slant a little toward his temples, like those of certain birds whose appearance he had assumed" (47).

It is precisely in Carpentier's treatment of the African slaves' belief in the supernatural powers of Mackandal that the problem of narrative perspective in his concept of marvelous realism becomes most evident. In the prologue to *El reino* Carpentier maintains that "the sensation of the marvelous presupposes faith. Those who do not believe in saints cannot be cured by the miracles of saints."[5] Since he does not share the religious beliefs of the slaves, how then can he portray the "marvelous" aspects of the Saint Domingue uprising without resorting to the same literary "tricks" for which he criticized the surrealists? His apparent solution is the mediating consciousness of Ti Noel, but his concept of faith as a prerequisite for the revelation of the marvelous still keeps him from fully participating in that consciousness; therefore, he must always present the perspective of the Saint Domingue slave in the third person. This narrative choice creates a sense of ironic distance that seems to undermine the author's concept of the marvelous in *El reino*.

Carpentier's account of Mackandal's execution ("The Great Flight" 1, vii) is an attempt to explain just how the Saint Domingue slaves may have come to believe in Mackandal's immortality, an explanation that would have been unnecessary of course if the narrative had been related entirely from the perspective of Ti Noel. The reader is informed that after Mackandal is tied to the stake and a fire is lit for his execution, the rebel appears to break loose from the post. In the commotion that follows, the slaves, who have been escorted to the square to witness this spectacle, do not see the colonial guards throw Mackandal back into the flames. Thus they remain firm in their belief in the maroon rebel's immortality and power of metamorphosis and return to their plantations "laughing all the way" to the astonishment of their European masters:

> Macandal had kept his word, remaining in the Kingdom of This World. Once more the whites had been outwitted by the Mighty Powers of the Other Shore. And . . . Lenormand de Mezy commented with his devout wife on the Negroes' lack of feelings at the torture of one of their own—drawing therefrom a number of philosophical considerations on the inequality of the human races which he planned to develop in a speech larded with Latin quotations. (52–53)

Irlemar Chiampi cites the epigraph to the prologue as an example of Carpentier's interest in establishing the rational basis of apparently supernatural phenomena. The epigraph, which is taken from Cervantes, reads: "What one must understand about this thing of people turning into wolves [lycanthropy] is that there is an illness doctors call *mania lupina*."[6] The premise that there is a rational explanation for the supernatural thus constitutes the realist aspect of *lo real maravilloso*, or the combination of the real and the marvelous that governs the constant interaction of myth and history in *El reino*.

Historically the spirit of Mackandal does indeed return some thirty-odd years later in the form of Bouckman, a slave originally from Jamaica who initiated the general insurrection in 1791 that would be carried on by Toussaint L'Ouverture, Henri Christophe, and Jacques Dessalines.[7] This time the call of the conch shells resounded from every corner of the island and changed the course of history. Saint Domingue would no longer be compared to the idyllic paradise of Bernardin de Saint-Pierre's *Paul et Virginie*.

Almost two years after the Declaration of the Rights of Man in Paris, one stormy night in August, Bouckman and his followers met in the forest of Bois Caiman where, after invoking the powers of the great Loas of Africa, they organized the rebellion that would gain them their freedom; within six weeks nearly all of the plantations of the Plaine du Nord were destroyed by fire. Although Bouckman was ultimately captured and beheaded on the very same spot where Mackandal was burned at the stake, the uprising he set in motion had far greater impact than the latter's visionary "march of poison." In order to gain control of Saint Domingue, Bouckman gambled on military support from France's enemies, the Spanish colonists in the western part of the island. That support was not forthcoming, but his successor Toussaint L'Ouverture was able to take advantage of the conflicts that arose among the metropolitan French, the white creole slaveholders, and the free people of color in the aftermath of the French Revolution.[8]

In Carpentier's fictional account of these events, it is only after the devastation of Bouckman's insurrection that the slaveholders understand the role of the religious practices of the slaves. Ti Noel's master Lenormand de Mezy comes to the realization that the rituals he held in contempt had brought about his ruin:

> It filled him with uneasiness, making him realize that, in certain cases, a drum might be more than just a goatskin stretched across a hollow

32

log. The slaves evidently had a secret religion that upheld and united them in their revolts. Possibly they had been carrying on the rites of this religion under his very nose for years and years, talking with one another on the festival drums without his suspecting a thing. But could a civilized person have been expected to concern himself with the savage beliefs of people who worshipped a snake. (78–79)

The invocation of the African loas Ogun (god of war) and Damballah (serpent god of fertility, mediator between heaven and earth) proved powerful weapons against the "civilized" decadence of the slaveholders and the European "Goddess of Reason." In *El reino* Carpentier suggests that the Europeans' failure to understand the role of vodun stemmed from their general contempt for the humanity of the slaves. Blinded by their own sense of superiority, the colonists dismissed the religious practices of the slaves as barbaric superstitions. The colonists failed to see that the African religious myths were symbolic expressions of the slaves' basic human values and historic experiences, which they would transform into a political quest for freedom.

The heroic-mythical phase of Carpentier's narrative reaches its climax with the execution of Bouckman and is followed by a transitional chapter in which the author deals with the emigration of the Saint Domingue plantation owners to Santiago de Cuba in the aftermath of the slave revolt. Thus Carpentier shifts the focus of the narrative away from the island of Saint Domingue at one of the most historically crucial moments of the revolution—the ascendancy of Toussaint L'Ouverture (1791–1802). In this chapter (2, v) Carpentier takes up two aspects of his concept of marvelous realism: the process of transculturation and New World baroque. This section of the novel reflects the research he carried out for *La música en Cuba* (1946), a scholarly work in which he shows the cultural impact of the migration of the French colonists, with many of their slaves, to cities such as Santiago. The colonists—and the slaves they took with them—influenced almost every aspect of the social and cultural life of the city, but their major contribution was the traditional music and dance forms that had developed in Saint Domingue and were later incorporated into Cuban music.[9]

In regard to his notion of the essentially baroque character of New

World art forms, Carpentier includes a scene in this chapter in which the eighteenth-century Cuban composer Esteban Salas conducts one of his *"sinfonías discordantes"* in the Cathedral of Santiago. The baroque atmosphere of the church reminds Ti Noel of the vodun temples of his homeland:

> The baroque golds, the human hair of the Christs, the mystery of the richly carved confessionals, the guardian dog of the Dominicans, the dragons crushed under saintly feet, the pig of St. Anthony, the dubious color of St. Benedict, the black Virgins, the St. Georges with the buskins and corselets of actors in French tragedies, the shepherds' instruments played on Christmas Eve had an attraction, a power of seduction in presence, symbols, attributes, and signs similar to those of the altars of the *houmforts* consecrated to Damballah, the Snake god. Besides, Saint James is Ogoun Fai, marshal of the storms, under whose spell Bouckman's followers had risen. (86–87)

Here at the very center of his narrative, Carpentier underscores the historical and cultural connections between the Caribbean islands and the process of cultural syncretism that inform his own literary project.

After the Santiago episode, Carpentier again takes up the historical events in Saint Domingue, but this time from the oblique perspective of Pauline Bonaparte, favorite sister of Napoleon and wife of General Leclerc. The latter was sent by Napoleon in 1801 to get rid of Toussaint L'Ouverture and to restore the institution of slavery to the island. The black general had declared himself governor and issued a declaration of independence from France.[10] Yet there is only the most indirect reference in *El reino* to the victories of Toussaint during this period (90). Undoubtedly any attempt to include Toussaint would have given an entirely different thrust to the narrative. By shifting the focus of history to the lesser-known, secondary figure Pauline Bonaparte, Carpentier highlights one of the major themes of *El reino*. The self-centered, licentious Pauline, who fancies herself "part Virginia, part Atala," is totally insensitive to the urgency of the political events taking place all around her. She is portrayed as the epitome of European decadence and immorality. In a later essay on marvelous realism, Carpentier writes that Pauline Bonaparte was *"lazarillo y guía"* (blindman's guide) in his investigation of just how the Age of Reason *enlightened* the Americas.[11]

The ideological premises against which Carpentier's narrative operates are the European concepts of civilization and history. Throughout *El reino* the myths, legends, and religious beliefs of the African slaves function in ideological counterpoint to the philosophic doctrines of the Age of Reason and the corruption of the ideals of the French Revolution. For Carpentier the concept of political freedom in its truest sense originates in the rebellions of Mackandal and Bouckman and not in the abstract philosophical principles of eighteenth-century Europe.[12]

In his interpretation of the defeat of the European plantocracy as a victory of the African gods, Carpentier shows the limitations of "narrow rationalist" conceptions of historical change.[13] Similarly, he interprets Henri Christophe's idolatry of European culture and contempt for the traditional values of the Haitian peasantry in the aftermath of the Revolution as a failure of vision that leads to yet another insurrection. Christophe's obsession with building monuments of achievement in the European style blinds him to the values and aspirations of his people just as it did the creole planters and the French.

Henri Christophe rose from slavery to become a military leader during the Revolution and proclaimed himself king of the northern region of Haiti in 1811. In Carpentier's novel, the protagonist Ti Noel returns from Santiago de Cuba to an independent Haiti to witness the final days of Christophe's reign. The former slave encounters omens of disaster everywhere in a landscape ravaged by historic struggles. But to his astonishment, in the midst of all the ruin and devastation emerges the "sumptuous pleasure garden" of Sans Souci, architectural symbol of Christophe's vision of creating an empire to rival that of the Europeans:

> Against a background of mountains violet-striped by deep gorges, rose a rose-colored palace, a fortress with ogival windows, rendered almost ethereal by the high socle of its stone stairway. To one side stood long-roofed sheds that were probably workshops, barracks, stables. To the other stood a round building crowned by a cupola resting on white columns where surpliced priests went in and out. As he drew nearer, Ti

Noel could make out terraces, statues, arcades, gardens, pergolas, artificial brooks, and boxwood mazes. At the foot of heavy columns, which supported a great sun of black wood, two bronze lions stood guard. Across the main esplanade white-uniformed officers busily came and went, young captains in bicornes, reflecting the glitter of the sun, sabers rattling on their thighs. (113–14)

Christophe's palace guards introduce Ti Noel to a new kind of tyranny; he discovers that in the land where "slavery had been abolished forever," the new ruler had instituted a system of forced labor to carry out his dreams of empire. So an aging Ti Noel is enlisted among the workers who haul the stones for the Citadel La Ferrière, Christophe's fortress high above the cliffs overlooking the Plaine du Nord.

Confident that his people share his visions of greatness, Christophe cynically manipulates their faith in the old gods by performing a ritual sacrifice of bulls and afterward mixing the blood with the mortar for the walls of the fortress, supposedly to make it invulnerable to attack. The king speculates that once his people have forgotten the suffering they have endured for its construction, they will look up at the magnificent citadel and see a king of their own race waiting "close to heaven . . . for the thud of the bronze hoofs of Ogoun's ten thousand horses" (125). Yet Christophe, surrounded by the trappings of European culture, remained aloof from the gods of Mackandal and Bouckman.

The Haitian ruler's legendary ambition and bold imagination are undermined by his despotism and insensitivity to his people. From the throne room of Sans Souci, Ave Marias mingle with the sound of vodun drums in the hills, and the people whose beliefs he had spurned set fire to his estates: "Henri Christophe, the reformer, had attempted to ignore Voodoo, molding with whiplash a caste of Catholic gentlemen. Now he realized that the real traitors to his cause that night were St. Peter with his keys, the Capuchins of St. Francis, the blackamoor St. Benedict along with the dark-faced Virgin in her blue cloak, and the Evangelists whose books he had ordered kissed each time the oath of loyalty was sworn" (148–49). The failure of Christophe's notion of historical progress is symbolized by his burial in the walls of the citadel; his impregnable fortress becomes the tomb or prison of his own static visions.[14]

In contrast to Christophe's rejection of the cultural traditions of his people, Ti Noel as historical witness and bearer of the collective memory remains faithful to the legacy of Mackandal and Bouckman, who had revolted against the "despair of peoples carried into captivity to build pyramids, towers, or endless walls" (48). That legacy is the positive link to the past that sustains the Haitian people in their struggle for freedom, whether it is directed against the Europeans or a "man of their own race" such as Christophe.

In the days of Mackandal, Ti Noel had begun to sense that he had a mission to fulfill. Although he has only a vague recollection of the things related to him by the one-armed rebel and is not sure what legacy has been passed down to him, he feels that it must be "something great, something commensurate with the rights acquired by one whose days had been so long on the earth" (171). So the old man takes to walking in the middle of the road with his arms wide open, talking incessantly, and he is greeted with signs of reverence as if he were Christ.

Although Carpentier expresses the fusion of myth and history through the consciousness of Ti Noel, the manifestations of the marvelous in *El reino* are often ironic, verging on caricature and parody. On his return to Haiti after nearly thirty years in Cuba, there seems to be an intensification in Ti Noel's capacity to experience premonitions, visions, and miracles; that is, the marvelous as defined by Carpentier in the prologue. He is said to have "acquired the art of talking with chairs, pots, a guitar, even a cow or his own shadow" (108). Yet the fact that this heightened sense of communion with all things occurs in his old age suggests the possibility of senility as much as any "privileged revelation of reality" based on faith in the supernatural.[15]

There is also an element of caricature in Carpentier's portrayal of Ti Noel in the period following the insurrection against Christophe. Having participated in the sacking and looting of the king's palace, Ti Noel carries off household items and transforms the ruins of the Lenormand de Mezy manor house into a "bizarre" Sans Souci. His prized possession, though, is a dress coat that had belonged to Christophe. At a festival of the drums Ti Noel is possessed by the spirit of the King of Angola, and the old man begins to imitate the ways of kings in what seems to be a parody of the regal airs of Christophe:

> Seated in his armchair, his coat unbuttoned, his straw hat pulled down to his ears, slowly scratching his bare belly, Ti Noel issued orders to the wind. But they were the edicts of a peaceable government, inasmuch as no tyranny of whites or Negroes seemed to offer a threat to his liberty. The old man filled the gaps in the tumbledown walls with fine things, appointed any passer-by a minister, any hay-gatherer a general, distributing baronetcies, presenting wreaths, blessing the little girls, and awarding flowers for services rendered. It was thus the Order of the Bitter Broom had come into being, the Order of the Christmas Gift, the Order of the Pacific Ocean, and the Order of the Nightshade. But the most sought after was the Order of the Sunflower, which was the most decorative. (172)

One of the key ironic images in this section of *El reino* is that of Ti Noel sitting on three volumes of the *Grande Encyclopédie*, eating sugarcane. This comic juxtaposition is obviously intended to show how insignificant the writings of the philosophers of the Enlightenment are for the concrete reality of the former slaves of Saint Domingue. As Carpentier insists again and again in *El reino*, the Saint Domingue tradition of freedom originates in the rebellion of Mackandal and the Declaration of Bois Caiman. Most of *El reino* is therefore based on the ironic contrast of Haitian folk beliefs and European rationalism, emphasizing the discrepancy between rationalist philosophical theories and historical reality.

In the final chapters of *El reino*, Carpentier allows himself to participate more directly in the mythic imagination of the protagonist Ti Noel. Ironic distance gives way to a process of mythopoesis. When historical conflict once more intrudes into his world, Ti Noel takes refuge in the memory of Mackandal and enters his own cycle of metamorphoses. This time, however, the various phases of transformation function as parables of human social relationships.

After the death of Christophe, Ti Noel discovers that all of Haiti is now under the control of the Republican mulattoes. As hundreds of peasants flee into the hills to escape the imposed labor of the new regime, he realizes that neither Mackandal nor Bouckman had fore-seen this turn of events: "The old man began to lose heart at this endless return of chains, this rebirth of shackles, this proliferation of suffering, which the more resigned began to accept as proof of the uselessness of all revolt" (177–78). Ti Noel decides to give up the "human guise" that had brought with it so much suffering. Like Mackandal he transforms himself into a bird, a stallion, a wasp, and even an ant, which he quickly realizes is a mistake since he ends up "carrying heavy loads over interminable paths under the vigilance of big-headed ants who remind him unpleasantly of Lenormand de Mezy's overseers, Henri Christophe's guards, and the mulattoes of today" (179).

In the final phase of Ti Noel's cycle of metamorphoses, Carpentier introduces the theme of utopia. The old man observes a clan of geese from the barnyards of Sans Souci, and since he admires the intel-ligence and orderliness of their communal life, he changes himself into one of their species only to be refused access to the rites and duties of the clan. Ti Noel is treated with contempt because he is an outsider:

> The clan now seemed a community of aristocrats, tightly closed against anyone of a different caste. The Great Gander of Sans Souci would have refused to have anything to do with the Great Gander of Dondon. Had they met face to face, hostilities would have ensued. Thus Ti Noel quickly gathered that even if he persisted in his efforts for years, he would never be admitted in any capacity to the rites and duties of the clan. It had been made crystal clear to him that being a goose did not imply that all geese were equal. No known goose had sung or danced the day of Ti Noel's wedding. None of those alive had seen him hatched out. He presented himself, without proper family back-ground, before geese who could trace their ancestry back four genera-tions. In a word, he was an upstart, an intruder. (183–84)

Since Ti Noel's cycle of metamorphoses does not provide escape from the harsh realities of injustice and oppression, it would appear that Carpentier is denying not only the possibility of utopia but the power of the mythic imagination as well. The parable of the clan of geese, however, reveals the other relationship between myth and history—the transformative power of myth conditioned by concrete

39

historical experience. Ultimately Ti Noel understands his rejection by the geese as punishment for having betrayed the legacy of Mackandal; the rebel slave had undergone a series of metamorphoses to *serve* his people, not to forsake the world of men. The true power of the mythical world of his African forefathers is the capacity to inspire hope in "the possible germinations the future held" (184).

Ti Noel's quest for freedom therefore cannot be resolved in a utopian transcendence of historical conflict. It is nevertheless a necessary and worthwhile quest since, as his experience teaches him, "In the Kingdom of Heaven there is no grandeur to be won, inasmuch as there all is established hierarchy, the unknown is revealed, existence is infinite, there is no possibility of sacrifice, all is rest and joy. For this reason, bowed down by suffering and duties, beautiful in the midst of his misery, capable of loving in the face of afflictions and trials, man finds his greatness, his fullest measure, only in the Kingdom of This World" (185). With this realization, Ti Noel's faith in the spirit of Bois Caiman is renewed. Since he now understands that each cycle of repression must be met with rebellion, he hurls an oath of defiance against the new masters.

El reino concludes with a hurricane—*"un gran viento verde"*—that sweeps across the Plaine du Nord, carrying off everything in its path, including the volumes of the *Encyclopédie* and the other remains of the Lenormand de Mezy plantation. Ti Noel disappears forever but the image of a vulture flying toward the thickets of Bois Caiman indicates the possibility of rebirth, a renewal of the quest for freedom.

As in *El reino*, the relationship between myth and history in Wilson Harris's "Guiana Quartet" is examined within the context of the struggle for liberation. Each of the novels of the Quartet series deals with the relentless exploitation of the land and its people in the history of the New World.[16] Although one of the central questions posed in the Quartet is "who are the rightful heirs of the land?", Harris interprets the issue of exploitation and freedom in broader metaphysical terms than does Carpentier in *El reino*. The historical fact of conquest, slavery, and indenture is an ever-present force in the Quartet, but Harris is concerned with the exploitative nature of personal relationships and enslavement to material fetishes of all kinds in the pursuit of "progress and profit." Consequently, the temporal world is depicted in these novels as "a graveyard of sculptured history and misadventure," and freedom is only possible through "alterations in the textures of the imagination"; or, as Harris describes this process in "History, Fable and Myth," "the psychic re-assembly of the dismembered god or gods."[17]

The Secret Ladder (1963), last novel of the Quartet, is closest to *El reino* in theme and subject matter since it deals specifically with the situation of the descendants of African slave rebels—the maroons— in modern Guyana. The novel was published during the period of extreme political upheaval that preceded Guyanese independence in 1966. On the eve of independence, over a hundred years after the abolition of slavery (1837), the maroons had still not been integrated into the social fabric of Guyanese society. They, like the Amerindian population, were still the object of exploitation and misunderstanding, a circumstance that threatened the future development of the country.

The figure of the maroon in *The Secret Ladder* represents the dismembered, repressed consciousness of the racially divided Guyanese past and present. Though rooted in the concrete historical reality of the period, Harris's novel is a highly symbolic juxtaposition of inner and outer frames of reality intended to subvert a uniform understanding of historical circumstance. Since Harris considers the subconscious imagination a more reliable indication of reality than the causal relationships of external events, plot is subordinate to the representation of consciousness in *The Secret Ladder*. Consequently time is relative to the subjective experience of the flux of those events. The narrative therefore takes place over a scant period of seven days but has symbolic resonances that cover some two hundred years of Guyanese history.

The confrontation between the forces of history and consciousness is set in the Amazon basin of equatorial Guyana on the Canje River, where Russell Fenwick, a young surveyor, has set up camp to take tidal readings for a government project to flood the land of a maroon community in the river district in order to provide irrigation for the East Indian rice farmers and the European sugarcane planters on the coast. The introspective Fenwick likes to think of the rivers of Guyana "as the curious rungs in a ladder on which one sets one's musing foot again and again, to climb into both the past and future of the continent of mystery" (151–52). But the rivers of the Guyana high-lands, clogged with the encroaching vegetation of the rain forest, are as difficult to maneuver as the ascent and descent of history.

Fenwick feels trapped in the monotonous passage of time that is marked hour after hour on the river gauge. He experiences the oppressive atmosphere of the rain forest as an "eternal primitive condition" that intensifies his feelings of self-doubt about his position as officer in charge of the surveying team. His inner chaos is reflected in the ever-changing features of the jungle landscape:

> An air of enormous artifice rested everywhere, the gnarled shadow of cloaked branches, naked leaves pinned fortuitously to the sky, these worn materials of earth stretched almost to the limits of enduring apprehension. Fenwick wanted to brush his thoughts aside. They were needling him into supplication, making him conscious of the imma-terial thread of awareness he possessed of the nature of himself, and other creatures and men. All was an artifice of mystery to which one addressed oneself often with idle and pretentious words. The shape of the mystery was always invisibly there, each representation the endless source of both humility and parody. Nothing lasted that did not show how soon it would crumble again. (195)

Fenwick's disorientation in space and time is further exacerbated by the disturbing presence of Poseidon, descendant of an African rebel slave and leader of the Canje River community. Although Fen-wick denies it, the old black man with the Greek name knows that the surveyor's work is part of a government plan to expropriate his land. At first Fenwick rejects Poseidon's role as the "black king of history," but the old man becomes an obsession, an ancestral ghost who haunts his waking and sleeping hours: "Here was the ambivalent *lapis* of all their hopes of ultimate freedom and archetypal authority as well as the viable symbol of inexhaustible self-oppression" (164–65). The young surveyor has a dream about a riderless, decapitated mare prancing in the midst of a group of horses on the edge of the savan-nah. The significance of this strange vision is gradually revealed over the course of the seven days that follow his first encounter with Poseidon. The image of the old fisherman standing on the banks of the river, "his ancient feet webbed with grass and muck," recalls the Greek Poseidon and his Roman counterpart Neptune who had the power to make horses rise from the depths onto the waves of the sea, symbolically unleashing the blind forces of primordial chaos.

As Michael Gilkes points out in his analysis of *The Secret Ladder*, Poseidon represents the Jungian archetype of the unconscious, and as such is the key to psychic unity as well as the creative imagination: "The old Negro, Poseidon, is (like the old Arawak woman of *Palace of the Peacock*) an archetypal figure representing the Folk, and the discovery of his fragile, 'buried community' has deep psychological significances for Fenwick and his men. . . . The presence of Poseidon's 'buried community' is a silent reminder of the need to accommodate the Folk, the buried inner self." Within this context Gilkes interprets *The Secret Ladder* as a "shamanistic *rite de passage*."[18] Fenwick's encounter with Poseidon thus forces him to confront his inner conflicts, presumably the first step toward the "unity of heart and mind" that will take place over the seven days of the narrative. Nevertheless, the resolution of inner and outer conflict remain highly problematic at the end of the novel.

Since *The Secret Ladder* deals more explicitly with sociopolitical realities than any of the other novels of the Quartet, Fenwick's rite of passage has direct implications for Guyanese society as a whole. The young surveyor compares the seven days that follow his first encounter with Poseidon to the seven days of creation in the "oldest fable" (206). While this period of genesis is as Gilkes says the beginning of a process of psychic reintegration, on the historical level it involves a process of deconstruction, a dismantling of the "shells and skeletons" of the past. Harris thus establishes an inverse relationship between psychic growth and the notion of historical progress.

In this respect the major difference between *The Secret Ladder* and *El reino* is the role of the folk in the historical process itself. In *El reino* the folk are portrayed as powerful, even heroic, agents of their own struggle for liberation. Carpentier, like Harris, assumes the role of mythmaker, but he allows the Haitian slave rebels to express their own voice by including their myths, beliefs, and points of view in the narrative. As agents of the subconscious imagination, the folk in *The Secret Ladder* are little more than psychic projections of other characters; they remain inarticulate and powerless against the forces of history. Inasmuch as Fenwick recognizes Poseidon as the "emotional dynamic of liberation" (171), the reader only experiences the old man from the outside or through the eyes of other characters in the novel.[19]

As the animating force of the subconscious, Poseidon exposes the underlying conflicts of the racially mixed surveying team. Their responses to the maroon range from the cynical and repressive attitudes of the camp cook Jordan and the foreman Weng to Bryant's identification with the old man as a beloved grandfather. Fenwick's attitude, however, is more ambivalent.[20] His education and his upper-class background make it difficult for him to communicate with Poseidon; he finds the old man's speech and appearance "alien . . . painful and extreme" (158). Yet he realizes that Poseidon must be understood by his generation or they will reap their own destruction since "to *misconceive* the African . . . is to misunderstand and exploit him mercilessly and oneself as well" (171).

Though Fenwick struggles to assert his liberal ideas against the authoritarian violence of Jordan and Weng, he predicts Bryant's love for the old man will kill him. This is consistent with Harris's notion that the retrieval of the past—the reassembly of the ancestral gods—involves a sacrificial death before it is possible to arrive at the "threshold of consciousness leading to a new age" (193). It is in this sense that Poseidon is "hooked and nailed to a secret ladder of conscience" (156).

Fenwick confesses his uneasiness about his job and his meeting with Poseidon in a letter to his mother. The young surveyor is as ambivalent about his own family background as he is about Poseidon; he feels a mixture of both pride and guilt about his family origins. We learn that he is of African, European, and Amerindian descent, and has taken on the difficult survey job in the bush to earn enough money to pay off his widowed mother's mortgage in return for the sacrifices she has made to educate him abroad. The tone of the letter is self-conscious and tentative; Fenwick characterizes his writing style as grandiloquent, full of inconsistencies and self-dramatization, which seems an ironic reference to Harris's own penchant for the "inflation" of consciousness.

Despite his apparent confusion, Fenwick shows an awareness of the consequences of the racial divisions that govern the politics of modern Guyana and clearly sees the link between his encounter with Poseidon and the current sociopolitical situation of his country. Referring to the threat of rebellion by the Canje River people, he expresses hope that the confrontation will not lead to bloodshed but might instead clear the air and restore what they have all lost—"the authority and psyche of freedom" (172).

By the sixth day of the narrative, however, the conflict between Fenwick's crew and Poseidon's people reaches a violent climax. Fenwick discovers the night reader Chiung lying unconscious near the river gauge; he had been hit over the head by some Canje River men who left him for dead. Still shaken by the attack against Chiung, Fenwick questions the members of the crew the following morning to try to unravel the "circumstantial riddle" of what exactly happened that night. He vaguely remembers the shadowy presence of two people at the stelling (wooden pier) that he could not readily identify. He becomes obsessed with this seemingly insignificant point but speculates that "Facts were, perhaps, always obscure in the end" (240). This statement illustrates Harris's own attitude toward factual realism in the novel and historicism in general. In this respect, the final chapter of the novel addresses the problem of the reliability of histories.

When Fenwick approaches Jordan, the cook spurns his quest for clarity since he blames the unrest at the camp on the young surveyor's liberalism and concern with issues of morality and conscience. Fenwick then turns to Van Brock, who only has a confused memory of what happened that evening because he was suffering from a bout of malarial fever. Furthermore, the commotion at the stelling had awakened him from a dream about his grandmother, which he relates to Fenwick in vivid detail.

In the dream Van Brock recalled his hometown, a poor village situated between the estuaries of the Essequibo and Pomeroon rivers on the Atlantic coast. Since the village was below sea level, its inhabitants were in a constant struggle against the rising tides of the sea. But during the dry season when the estuaries turned to salt, the villagers engaged in what Van Brock describes as a daily ritual of disposing their "nightly pots" into a swamp before sunrise and then searching deep into the earth for fresh water. Van Brock dreams that on one such morning he inadvertently throws out his grandmother's gold ring with the waste. The old woman is grief stricken over the loss of the ring since it was her only remembrance of his grandfather, a Dutchman, who according to varying accounts drowned at sea or in the waterfalls of the interior. Infuriated by the old woman's despair, Van Brock callously abuses her and precipitates her death. As an act of penance, he descends into the filthy pit of waste to retrieve the ring and restores it to the dead woman's finger like "a dutiful priest at the wedding of memory" (246).

Van Brock's dream is a parable in which history is depicted as a "ritual of waste." His family myth about the "spirit of gold" with its legacy of abuse and guilt contains all the basic elements of the social history of the Guyanese people: the relentless struggle against the forces of nature, the mixed racial heritage, and above all the quest for worldly goods that laid the foundations of that history in the New World. Van Brock's query about whether his act of penance had created "an ancestor of life or death" repeats Harris's fundamental concern about the meaning of the past, which is the central focus of the novel as a whole.

Van Brock's account of his grandmother's death coincides with the arrival of Bryant and Catalena Perez who announce the death of Poseidon. Catalena, the wife of a crew member that Fenwick fired, had followed Bryant into the rain forest in search of the old man. When they found him and the other rebels gathered around their camp, Poseidon became enraged because he thought Catalena had betrayed him. Bryant intervened to protect her, accidently causing the old man to stumble and strike his head on the rim of a bucket. Poseidon lay crumpled on the ground in the shadow of a mare, murdered by "the grandson he had begotten in the dreadful apotheosis of history" (251); thus Fenwick's prophetic dream of the decapitated horse is fulfilled. Bryant and Catalena relate how they were threatened by Poseidon's men but saved by the sudden appearance of the "wild twins," the same men who had hit the night reader Chiung over the head.[21] The two men had returned to the camp to warn the rebels that the foreman of the survey team would be coming after them with the jungle police. Faced with the loss of their leader and threatened with repression, Poseidon's people give up their rebellion, bitterly resigned to the expropriation of their land for the government project.

Time, space, and sequence of events become increasingly dislocated in the narration of the final events of the novel. On the morning of the seventh day, Fenwick awakes from a strange dream in which "it seemed that an inquisition of dead gods and heroes had ended. . . . The one chosen from amongst them to descend was crying something Fenwick was unable to fathom but the echoes of annunciation grew on every hand and became resonant with life. . . . In our end . . . our end . . . our end is our beginning" (258–59). Poseidon's spirit cries out in Fenwick's dream like the voice of Merlin in exile, suggesting as Harris does in a reference to the Jungian interpretation of the fate of the legendary magician and prophet "that he lives on in unredeemed form. His story is not yet finished, and he still walks abroad."[22] *The Secret Ladder* concludes—as does *El reino de este mundo*—with a vision of sacrifice and an invocation of the possibility of regeneration. For Carpentier, however, the mythic pattern of rebirth is related to an affirmation of the quest for freedom within the historical process itself, since as Ti Noel discovers "in the Kingdom of Heaven there is no grandeur to be won." But since Harris rejects the "material vision of time," in *The Secret Ladder* freedom is only possible in the realm of inner consciousness, and above all in the arts of the imagination.

The maroon rebel as quimboiseur—healer, visionary, and story-teller—is the central figure in the French Caribbean writer Edouard Glissant's novel *Le quatrième siècle* (1964). Papa Longoué, last descendant of an African maroon who seized his freedom on the very first day of arrival in the New World, is the "Master of the Night," but his status as seer and bearer of historical knowledge is challenged, like that of Poseidon in *The Secret Ladder,* by young Mathieu Béluse, future historian and political activist in post–World War II Martinique.

Le quatrième siècle opens with the quimboiseur's evocation of the rising wind of a destructive hurricane, which like the sea is associated with memory. For Papa Longoué historical knowledge is the vertiginous descent into an obscure past, a knowledge beyond words:

47

Parce que le passé n'est pas dans ce que tu connais par certitude, il est
aussi dans tout ce qui passe comme le vent et que personne n'arrête
dans ses mains fermées.

(Because the past is not just in what you know for certain but it is also
in everything that goes by like the wind and that no one can hold back
with closed hands.)[23]

Papa Longoué conjures up the living past, eschewing logic, evidence,
and clarity. His method is the art of divination, uncovering the
hidden signs, *les traces*, in the fragmented, disorderly accumulation of
events that constitute the African experience in the New World.
Mathieu's project is to explore this "obscure chronicle," testing the
powers of logic against the quimboiseur's magic.

When Mathieu asks Papa Longoué to tell him about the past,
he begins an inquiry into the very nature of history and historical
change. Glissant contrasts the quimboiseur's intuitive vision with
Mathieu's penchant for documents and chronologies. As a direct
descendant of the African ancestor who rejected slavery, Papa Longoué is identified with myth. Like Carpentier in *El reino*, Glissant
reclaims the mythic function of the maroon as cultural symbol of
rebellion and possibility in Caribbean history. But myth also functions in the text as a form of consciousness, a way of knowing that
Mathieu is inclined to dismiss as magic or sorcery. Neither Papa
Longoué's "magic" nor Mathieu's book learning, however, are suffi-
cient in themselves. Glissant suggests that historical understanding
can only be achieved through the dialogue between past and present
that takes place during their meetings in the legendary forest.

For Papa Longoué history does not begin in the sacred world of
African myth but with the arrival of two ancestors on the slave ship
Rose-Marie. This beginning is a moment of rupture, a moment that is
both an end and a beginning. Although Mathieu is obsessed with
establishing chronologies, he becomes impatient with the quimboiseur's slow, ritualized account of the first day, the *cérémonie de l'arri-
vage*. But the old man insists on the importance of marking the hours,
the order of events, on that first day (the only chronology he adheres
to), since time would become a luxury for the African captives;
perhaps a scrupulously detailed account of that first day might reveal

an opening, *une trouée*, toward something other than the horrors of the Middle Passage.

Through the quimboiseur's discourse with young Mathieu, Glissant constructs an intricate history based on the genealogy of the Longoué and Béluse families, separate bloodlines that eventually converge in the figure of Papa Longoué himself, the son of Apostrophe Longoué and Stéfanise Béluse. The original ancestors were shipmates and rivals whose experience in the New World represents the dual legacies of rebellion and domination. Like Papa Longoué's genealogy, history in *Quatrième* is a complex tangle that defies the concept of linear causality and simple dichotomies. As Apostrophe Longoué's name and marriage to Stéfanise Béluse indicate there is no pure, unbroken line of descent. History consists of gaps and sudden leaps rather than linear succession. The important question is not, therefore, as Mathieu repeatedly asks, why Longoué rebelled and Béluse did not, but what their different experiences tell us about present and future possibilities.

Despite Papa Longoué's elaborate genealogy, his evocation of the past is a story without a plot. Rather than the linear development of the traditional narrative, *Quatrième* is structured to accommodate the multiple voices and dispersed elements of historical experience. In this sense, the novel resembles the history called for by Mathieu in *La Lézarde:* "Write a story. . . . Write it like a river. Slow. Like the Lézarde. With rushing water, meanders, sometimes sluggish, sometimes running freely, slowly gathering the earth from either bank. Like that, yes, picking up the earth round it. Little by little. Like a river, murky with secrets that it deposits in the calm sea."[24]

In *Quatrième*, however, the whirlwind (*le tourbillon*) and the forest are the metaphors of Glissant's narrative method and concept of history. The novel not only questions the meaning of history but also how to write that history. The story is a chaotic spiral of repetitions, bits and pieces of narrative built up in a montage of interconnected lives and events in which past, present, and future merge. The dispersed, discontinuous elements of the text are a literal reflection of the psychic experience of rupture and fragmentation characteristic of Caribbean history. As Glissant points out in *Le discours antillais:*

Les Antilles sont le lieu d'une histoire faite de ruptures et dont le commencement est un arrachement brutal, la Traite. Notre conscience historique ne pouvait pas "sédimenter," si on peut ainsi dire, de manière progressive et continue, comme chez les peuples qui ont engendré une philosophie souvent totalitaire de l'histoire, les peuples européens, mais s'agrégeait sous les auspices du choc, de la contraction, de la négation douloureuse et de l'explosion. Ce discontinu dans le continu, et l'impossibilité pour la conscience collective d'en faire le tour, caractérisent ce que j'appelle une non-histoire.

(The West Indies is the site of historical ruptures, the beginning of which is a brutal uprooting, the Slave Trade. Our historical consciousness could not "sediment," if one can put it that way, in a progressive and continuous manner, as among peoples who have produced an often totalitarian philosophy of history, the Europeans, but it was aggregated under the auspices of shock, of contraction, of painful negation and of explosion. This discontinuity within continuity, and the impossibility of the collective consciousness to assess it, characterize what I call a non-history.)[25]

As if compelled to fill an alien space, the spiritual void of dispossession, with a dense "inextricable forest of words" (*Quatrième* 66), Glissant records nearly every aspect of the Africans' physical and psychological insertion into the New World: captivity on the Guinea Coast, the holds of the slave ship, the slave market, resistance and endurance, the slave hunt and dogs, shackles and whippings, the founding of families, the beginnings of a new language and culture. *Quatrième* is the account book, *le bilan*, as it were, of four hundred years of the European slave trade. Yet the adequacy of words to convey that history is questioned throughout the text.

With the aid of Papa Longoué, Mathieu digs through the "archives of memory" that have been effaced by the "absurd catalog of official history."[26] Retrieving the unwritten record of memory is only the beginning; meaning, like the story without a plot, must be constructed outside, or rather beyond the text, the written record. Nevertheless, the first step toward historical consciousness is the creative exploration of the past, in all its chaotic fragmentation, engaged in by Mathieu and Papa Longoué.

Through his discourse with the quimboiseur, Mathieu discovers a different way of measuring historical time:

Il avait commencé la chronologie et posé la première borne à partir de laquelle mesurer les siècles. Non pas l'écart de cent années déroulées l'une après l'autre, mais l'espace parcouru. . . . "La mer qu'on traverse, c'est un siècle." Oui, un siècle. Et la côte où tu débarques, aveuglé, sans âme ni voix, est un siècle. Et la forêt, entretenue dans sa force jusqu'à ce jour de ton marronnage . . . est un siècle. Non pas enrubannés dans l'artifice savant d'un tricentenaire, mais noués au sang méconnu, à la souffrance sans voix, à la mort sans écho. Etalés entre le pays infini et ce pays-ci qu'il fallait nommer, découvrir, porter; enfouis dans ces quatre fois cent ans . . . perdus dans le temps sans parole. (*Quatrième* 268–69)

(He had commenced the chronology and set the first boundary from which to measure the centuries. Not the span of a hundred years unfolded one after another, but the space traveled through. . . . "The sea that one crosses, is a century." Yes, a century. And the coast where you land, blind, without soul or voice, is a century. And the forest, whose power sustained you until that day of your marronnage . . . is a century. Not tied with ribbon in the erudite artifice of a tricentenary, but tied to unacknowledged blood, to voiceless suffering, to unechoed death. Stretched out between the infinite country and this country here that one had to name, to discover, to bear; buried in these four times one hundred years . . . lost in speechless time.)

The uprooted African's relationship to the land is central to an understanding of the past and the present. The text is not only an opportunity to bear witness to the beauty of an exploited and often trivialized landscape (variously described as paradise island and "speck of dust" in the Caribbean sea), but also is itself the space in which the land serves as a point of reference for the ordering of historical experience. The alienation of slavery is experienced as dislocation in time and space, the de-centered self strung out in a psychic and cultural void.

The example of the maroon is significant in this regard because unlike the slave, the rebel fugitive establishes his own relationship to the land and therefore actively participates in the making of his own history. When the first Longoué seizes the opportunity to escape on the first day of arrival, he enters a new history. He penetrates the unknown forest, combing the landscape and getting to know its every "root and branch" (*Quatrième* 104). The maroon ancestor is also known as La Pointe because of his frequent excursions to the coast where he looks out over the sea toward the land beyond the waters. Since he recognizes that there is no possibility of going back, he embraces this new land and prepares himself for a new life. The African rebel is reborn in the forest of marronnage. He preserves the memory of the lost homeland beneath the dense foliage of the forest, symbolically represented by the serpent coiled around the *tête de boue*, the head he fashions from the mud of the forest floor on that first night. Venturing into the unknown, the maroon replaces the primordial forest of Africa, *le pays infini*, with the forest of marronnage in the New World.

The opposition between the two ancestors, Longoué and Béluse, is expressed in their relationship to the land. While the maroon Longoué embraces the new land and begins a new life with a woman of his own choice, the "girl warrior" Louise whom he abducts from the La Roche plantation, the slave Béluse is dominated by the debauchery and physical presence of the slave master who controls every aspect of his life. Confinement, lack of choice, silent endurance, and above all imposed "uncreative" labor in a land he cannot claim as his own define the slave's existence. The two rivals are symbolic of the dual legacy of the African presence in the New World: resistance and endurance, engagement and alienation, self-determination and domination.

The mountain forests and the coastal plains are therefore associated with two different forms of consciousness. The forest is the space of memory and identity capable of engendering the future; the plains, the space of oblivion and degradation, *l'espace dégénéré*, where the land ceases to speak to you (*Quatrième* 129). Yet, as Papa Longoué points out to Mathieu, history "had flowed through the plains just as it had burst out over the hills." What is needed is a regeneration of consciousness, which like a volcanic eruption would reduce the forest/plains division to ashes, fertilizing the entire landscape (*Quatrième*

147). The people of the plains must assimilate the maroons' "rage of refusal" (*Quatrième* 231).

Young Mathieu Béluse dreams of establishing a new relationship to the land:

Car la terre . . . *n'est-ce pas toujours ce qui reste?* . . . il faudra bien qu'un jour ils la renversent sur elle-même, qu'elle donne son profit. . . . il faudra bien qu'un jour elle cesse de mentir, et que ceux qui la travaillent, loin d'aucune sorte de haute-parleur pour leur damnation sans fin, trouvent enfin l'éclaircie dans les bois. . . . Car c'est le Rôle et c'est l'Acteur, puisque tout ce qui par ailleurs est souffert et accompli ne l'est qu'en fonction d'elle, parce qu'elle existe et qu'elle permet qu'on reste debout juste assez pour ne pas mourir? . . . je te dis qu'ils vont la cultiver à la fin, la cultiver vraiment et non pas trimer sans raison tout au long de son corps. (*Quatrième* 189–90)

(For isn't the land . . . *all that is left?* . . . one day it will be necessary to turn it over, so that it can yield up its profits. . . . one day it must cease to lie, and those who work it, far from any kind of loud-speaker for their endless damnation, will finally find the light in the woods. . . . For it is the Part and it is the Actor, since isn't everything else suffered and accomplished only by means of it, because it exists and it lets you keep standing just long enough not to die? . . . I am telling you they're going to cultivate it at last, truly cultivate it and not wear themselves out on it senselessly.)

Mathieu is soon disillusioned, however, when he learns that the expanse of land at the edge of the forest belongs to Mr. Larroche. Nearly a hundred years after emancipation there has only been a superficial change, like the spelling of the La Roche family name, in the former slaves' relationship to the land. Alienation from the land, the small marginalized space of the Caribbean island as well as the African *pays infini*, is not resolved with the legal decrees of abolition but continued in the colonial and neocolonial situation of Caribbean societies in the twentieth century. Still in control of the land, the former slave masters, now benefactors of colonial rule, have "locked up the past" and the future, claiming history as theirs alone (*Quatrième* 182). After five years of regular visits with the quimboiseur, young Mathieu is able to grasp the connection between history and the land; but if he is unable to go beyond a purely abstract under-standing of that relationship, he will be trapped in the dilemma of the educated elite of a new generation who neither works the land nor owns it (*Quatrième* 284).

Mathieu's fiancée Mycéa, a distant relative of Papa Longoué, rec-ognizes the dangers of his obsession with the past:

> Elle pressentait que c'était mortel d'ignorer le vertige (en méconnais-sant ce qui l'engendrait) et mortel de s'y complaire sans fin. . . .
> . . . le fait est qu'il faut apprendre ce que nous avions oublié, mais que, l'apprenant, il nous faut l'oublier encore. (*Quatrième* 273, 285)

> (She sensed that it was fatal not to know the vertigo (by misunderstand-ing what it would engender) and fatal to indulge in it endlessly. . . .
> . . . the fact is we must learn what we have forgotten, but having learned it, we must forget it again.)

Mycéa understands that the purpose of remembering the past is to prepare oneself for the difficult task of constructing the future; she knows that history is not only what we have suffered but also what we create. As the spiritual children, the chosen descendants, of the Longoué legacy of refusal, Mathieu and Mycéa must repossess the land and claim their own space in history. This, of course, involves the political process, *l'acte fondamental*, of decolonization, the subject of Glissant's earlier novel *La Lézarde*.

Significantly, the death of the quimboiseur coincides with a crucial turning point in the history of the island. Papa Longoué dies during the political campaigns that led to the 1946 referendum that would result in the political integration of Martinique as an overseas depart-ment of metropolitan France. Historically and culturally, the 1946 referendum represents an erosion of the spirit of marronnage. The Longoué line of genealogical descent runs out and with it the living link to a past, which if repudiated "would in turn repudiate the new land" (*Quatrième* 286). The 1946 referendum is thus a betrayal that threatens the future possibility of a new history in Martinique.

All that remains of the Longoué family history is the contents of a sack that the old man sends to Mathieu before his death: an ebony carving of the original ancestor, the broken pieces of a barrel, and the dusty remains of a serpent. These relics of the past, like Pilate's bag of bones in Toni Morrison's *Song of Solomon,* are the unassimilated contents of historical memory that Mathieu's generation must reconstruct and translate into effective political action.

According to Glissant, the serpent, *la bête-longue,* haunts the subconscious of the people of Martinique.[27] In Carpentier's novel, *El reino,* the serpent is related to the West African religious beliefs that played such an important role in the slave rebellions of Haiti and is therefore symbolic of historical and cultural transformation. In *Quatrième* the meaning of the serpent is forgotten, buried at the bottom of a barrel where it turns to dust. Yet its presence is always lurking in the shadows of consciousness, lying in wait. For the African descendants of Martinique, the serpent is an object of fear rather than veneration.

Despite repeated references to the serpent, African myths and religious beliefs are alluded to in *Quatrième* but not related in the text. As a child the house slave Louise sneaks out at night to listen to the stories of the field slaves. Eventually they forbid her to join their storytelling sessions because of their fear of the slave master La Roche, and Louise is forced to listen secretly outside the walls of the slave quarters. Stories of Africa are "forbidden knowledge" on the plantations of the coastal plains.

Even among the rebellious maroons, memory of African cultural origins is imperfect, incomplete. The first Longoué is said to have shared as little as possible of his knowledge of Africa in order to bolster his own status. Papa Longoué, the last of the line, is described as a barely competent quimboiseur who *"n'avait jamais pu rien raccrocher à rien, ni son père à son fils, ni par conséquent le passé à l'avenir* [had never been able to connect anything, neither his father to his son, nor consequently the past to the future]" (*Quatrième* 19).

In *Quatrième* Glissant exploits the characteristically multiple, ambivalent meanings associated with the serpent as cultural symbol. The primordial serpent is identified with power and may be either a positive or negative force—one of transformation and rebirth or one of affliction and destruction.[28] There are, in fact, two serpents in the text—one associated with the African ancestor Longoué and the other with the European planter La Roche. When the Longoué ancestor first confronts his would-be slave master he makes a menacing ritual sign—tracing a serpent in the air. The sign of the serpent is the African "magic" he uses to ward off the evil powers of his captors. This magic succeeds because he is able to communicate the sign to the young creole slave, Louise, who helps him to escape into the woods. As the captain of the slave ship observes, the Africans were always able to "transmit some memory of their former state" (*Quatrième* 51) despite the planters' efforts to suppress their knowledge of the African past.

The maroon ancestor not only uses the powers of the serpent against La Roche but against his African shipmate Béluse as well. Once he finds safety in the forest, at dawn on the second day of arrival, the maroon's first act is to make a gnarled, reptilian figure from bits of wood and vine, which he coils around a head made from the red mud of the forest floor. At first he uses this clay image to render his rival shipmate "useless" on the plantation by thwarting his ability to father children:

> Il fallait peser sur l'autre, jusqu'à ce qu'il reste impuissant capon vivant sans raison acceptant la vie. (*Quatrième* 97)

> (It was necessary to lean heavily on the other, until he was left a powerless coward living senselessly, accepting life.)

He then claims to have removed the liana serpent and scattered the broken pieces of the *tête de boue,* making it possible for the Other to father the children of slavery, "the descendants he deserves" (*Quatrième* 109). Longoué is remarkably ambivalent toward both La Roche and Béluse, alternately cursing and protecting them. The fate of the maroon is inextricably bound to that of the plantation slave and the slave master.[29]

Ten years after his escape, the Longoué ancestor encounters his rival La Roche deep in the forest, where the planter has tracked him down to give him an ebony carving made in the maroon's own image and a small barrel; these are the relics that Papa Longoué sends to Mathieu before his death. The barrel contains a deadly serpent, the European's *renvoi,* his countersign, which he uses to turn the maroon's curse back against him. La Roche wants Longoué to carry the barrel with him wherever he goes and predicts that its presence will upset his descendants. Both the African and the European are cursed—the Longoué line destined to become "ever more tame" and the La Roche line to be "drowned in the stupefied scull of a cretin" (*Quatrième* 110). The barrel is kept by the Longoué family for over 150 years, continually patched up but never once opened until the serpent turns to dust.

La Roche acknowledges the African rebel as the "master of the heights"; the maroon, for his part, defers every opportunity to kill the European planter and never wages a full-scale rebellion of the kind carried out in Saint Domingue. The echoes of revolt in Saint Domingue resound throughout the Caribbean colonies, but the Martinique maroons only make brief incursions into the plains from time to time to help those who revolt on the plantation estates; the hills were the only place that belonged to them (*Quatrième* 94). Despite his bold refusal to accept slavery, the maroon is marginalized; his revolt is contained, locked up in the forest like the serpent in La Roche's barrel. Longoué repeatedly vows to settle accounts with La Roche at a later time, but that time never comes, either in his own life or in that of his descendants. As Mathieu would later observe *"c'est ça notre conte une longue file* d'autre fois *attachée avec des morts* [that's our story a long line of *some other times* strung together with dead people]" (*Quatrième* 121).

La Roche is himself a renegade who shuns the company of his own people for that of the blacks and brings the young slave girl, Louise, into his house as a cure for his own sense of spiritual damnation. He is fascinated by what the other planters consider the "demonic practices of the slaves," their knowledge of herbs, poisons, and magic potions. Mathieu, however, rejects the idea of La Roche as the "quimboiseur of the planters" (*Quatrième* 120). When he hears Papa Longoué's account of the meeting in the forest, he is angered by what appears to be a pact between the planter and the maroon. He criticizes Longoué's failure to open the barrel or even name what was in it, as if La Roche had the power to impose whatever content or meaning he wished on their history.

Thus La Roche appropriates the power of the African's sign and turns it against his descendants. The European planter's *renvoi* is symbolic of the repressed roots of historical consciousness. Yet the latent, explosive potential of the contents of the barrel always threatens to upset the surface accommodations of the Béluse and Longoué descendants who become colonial subjects and then "citizens" of France in 1946. The subconscious force of collective memory must become conscious rebellion. The dual symbolism of the serpent can only be resolved when the pact between the maroons and planters is put to an end. The maroons must come down from the hills, leaving behind the "forest of legends," so that the people of the plains can learn to set their own fires. With the death of the last maroon ancestor, the filial link is broken, but as in the case of Poseidon in *The Secret Ladder,* the maroon's story is not yet finished. Marronnage, even when defeated by the forces of history, is therefore a recurrent theme in Glissant's fiction. In his later novels the maroon rebel is a constant reminder of the need to make one's own history and forge a new relationship to the land.

In Caribbean fiction the historical fact of marronnage becomes a new form of mythic discourse that addresses the conflict between African and European belief systems, folk tradition and modernity, resistance and assimilation. For Carpentier the maroon rebel is a direct link to the African past, and as such preserves the mythologies that the Haitian slaves use to challenge the "outer frame" of history in concrete political ways. His use of the maroon legends in *El reino* was an act of cultural reappropriation related to his attempt to establish a poetics of the novel based on the folk traditions of New World culture. But as his ironic treatment of African religious beliefs in *El reino* indicates, the author's search for literary and cultural authenticity remains problematic. Unlike Carpentier, both Harris and Glissant emphasize cultural divergence and discontinuity. In their novels, they point to the dangers of idealizing the maroon and the African past, but they also recognize the need to understand the maroon in order to bring the repressed knowledge of the past into historical consciousness.

PART TWO

The Problematic
Quest for Origins

C H A P T E R   3

The Myth of El Dorado:
Los pasos perdidos and
Palace of the Peacock

In Carpentier's *Los pasos perdidos* (*The Lost Steps*, 1953) and Harris's *Palace of the Peacock* (1960), Latin American and Caribbean history is the context of a search for cultural and personal identity. The basic similarity between *Lost Steps* and *Palace* is the evocation of the history of the European conquest and the search for gold in the sixteenth and seventeenth centuries. This is symbolically represented in the quest motif of the legend of El Dorado. The protagonists of both novels travel backward through time as they work their way upriver to the interior of a South American jungle. By means of this symbolic journey, Carpentier and Harris are able to interweave the modern theme of alienation with Western, Oriental, and native American mythology. The historical and mythical elements function quite differently, however, in the two novels.

In his study of mythopoesis, Harry Slochower points out that modern mythopoeic works tend to arise in periods of crisis or cultural transition, offering the writer a means of overcoming depersonalization and alienation.[1] His definition of mythopoesis as the re-creation and *transformation* of the traditional patterns of myth is applicable to the literature of the colonial and postcolonial societies of the Caribbean. Among Caribbean writers the quest for origins—the central problem inscribed in myth—arises precisely when their societies are faced with the transition from the colonial past to independence. This transition is complicated by a multiple heritage that is often interpreted as a lack of tradition since it does not fit the mold of Old World patterns. The question of filiation thus becomes an issue of cultural legitimacy and authority.

Slochower's description of mythopoesis as "*a drama* in three acts, followed by *an epilogue*" is similar to Harris's concept of the novel as a "drama of consciousness." In modern mythopoesis the state of communal harmony associated with paradise or the golden age of Genesis in traditional myth is only "a nostalgic memory."[2] For the Caribbean writer this is expressed as a longing for what Wilson Harris calls a "tribal past."[3] Given the multicultural heritage of the peoples of the Caribbean, the problem becomes which "tribal past"—the Amerindian, the African, or the European? On a more personal level, this problem may be expressed as the writer's longing for an initial state of harmony before a present condition of cultural alienation from his or her community.

According to Slochower, in modern mythopoesis the traditional pattern of the quest assumes the form of a challenge to the existing social order in which the protagonist—a hero of ambiguous status—must undergo a process of self-examination before becoming the "creative agent of his community"; and the protagonist's quest "points to a futuristic order which is envisaged as integrating the valuable residues of the past and present."[4] Among Caribbean writers this drama of consciousness is presented as a challenge to the social relationships determined by the history of the conquest and colonialism, and is a process in which the heroes or heroines must confront their own social and cultural alienation.[5]

In the modern mythopoeic work the reintegration of the protagonist (the homecoming) and the resolution of conflict is usually problematic, since historical reality precludes the "paradisiac finale" of traditional myth.[6] The "victory" of consciousness must be reconquered over and over again, which accounts for the frequent recurrence of the quest theme not only in Caribbean literature but also in literature in general, even in those works that claim to be only about the writing process itself.

In most respects, Carpentier's and Harris's use of the mythical framework of a river journey toward the spiritual El Dorado of the interior follows Slochower's description of the process of my-thopoesis and involves a revision of the pattern of separation, exile, and return in traditional myth. In *Lost Steps* and *Palace of the Peacock*, the legend of El Dorado functions as a link between the past and the present. By reenacting the quest for El Dorado, the protagonists of the two novels are able to lay claim to their personal and collective pasts, giving new meaning to their present. In *Lost Steps*, for example, the protagonist becomes absorbed in the mythical past one evening as he and his companions are sitting around a campfire on the periphery of the interior. While listening to the tales of the herbal doctor Montsalvatje, he recognizes the similarity between his journey and that of the original seekers of El Dorado:

> We all felt an impulse to rise, set out, and arrive before the dawn at the gateway of enchantment. Again the waters of Lake Parima gleamed. Once more the towers of Manoa arose. The possibility that they might exist came alive anew, inasmuch as the myth persisted in the imagination of all those who lived in the vicinity of the jungle—that is to say, of the Unknown. And I could not help thinking that Adelantado, the Greek miners, the two rubbergatherers, and all those who each year made their way into the heart of its darkness after the rains, were, in fact, seeking El Dorado, like those who first followed the lure of its name.[7]

The musing narrator of *Palace of the Peacock* suggests a similar correspondence:

> The map of the savannahs was a dream. The names Brazil and Guiana were colonial conventions I had known from childhood. I clung to them now as to a curious necessary stone and footing, even in my dream, the ground I knew I must not relinquish. They were an actual stage, a presence, however mythical they seemed to the universal and the spiritual eye. They were as close to me as my ribs, the rivers and the flatland, the mountains and the heartland I intimately saw. I could not

help cherishing my symbolic map, and my bodily prejudice like a well-known room and house of superstition within which I dwelt. I saw this kingdom of man turned into a colony and battle ground of spirit, a priceless tempting jewel I dreamed I possessed.[8]

In parallel reinterpretations of the legend of El Dorado, the search for primitive instruments in *Lost Steps* and the pursuit of the Amerindians in *Palace* lead the protagonists to the "frontier of the known and the unknown," toward a repossession of self in the heart of the rain forest.

A brief examination of the legend of El Dorado illustrates the interrelationship of myth and history in the consciousness of New World writers and reveals the complex symbolism associated with it. El Dorado is emblematic of the first encounter of the European and the Amerindian, the Old and the New World. Furthermore, this nexus of myth and history reveals how vision—the idealism of the quest—was corrupted by the realism of the conquest.

Irlemar Chiampi includes El Dorado as one of the five great legends of the New World.[9] The mythical kingdom of El Dorado was thought to be located somewhere between the Amazon and Peru. The legend is said by some to have originated among the Chibcha Indians, who once a year anointed their king with oil and powdered him with gold dust, which he then washed off in a sacred lake, simultaneously throwing offerings of emeralds and gold into the waters. This ancient religious rite died out long before the arrival of the Europeans, but the legend of a land of gold and plenty lived on, giving impetus to a series of expeditions in the sixteenth and seventeenth centuries.[10]

The most famous of these expeditions were carried out by the Spaniards Antonio de Berrio and Domingo de Vera and the Englishman Walter Raleigh. The English courtier and soldier of fortune made two voyages in search of the kingdom of El Dorado. The first expedition in 1595 took him some three hundred miles up the Orinoco River. His account of this voyage was published as *The Discoverie of the lovlie, rich and beautiful Empyre of Guiana with a relation of the great city of Manoa (which the Spanyards call El Dorado)*, London, 1596. His second attempt to find the fabled City of Gold in 1617 brought him into conflict with the Spaniards, who were already established on the South American mainland, and this latter episode ultimately cost him his life.[11]

The return to the legend of El Dorado by writers as varied as Carpentier, Harris, and Naipaul indicates the persistent need of Caribbean writers to examine the origins of New World history and culture. The picture that emerges is a complex one fraught with contradictory signs. El Dorado is both a place and an object of desire; it is a symbol of paradise lost and utopia, a symbol of rupture and the promise of fulfillment. The search for fulfillment on both a material and a spiritual level and the promise of a new beginning in the "marvelous" landscape of the South American interior, however, involved a confrontation with its Amerindian inhabitants, who were alternately denigrated and idealized in the minds of the Europeans.

The dynamics of this initial encounter are at the root of the Caribbean writer's quest for cultural identity and a literary tradition to express it. Like the African slave, the Amerindian becomes the focus of a cultural dilemma; that is, the cultural alienation of the intellectual suspended in limbo between two worlds—the Amerindian or African paradise lost and the world of the European conquest. Many Caribbean writers have felt compelled to choose between the two, while some like Harris and Carpentier have sought an accommodation. But as Harris puts it, there is "no easy intercourse with tradition,"[12] in this sense history and historical conflict. Thus rupture, alienation, and the desire for communion (the true object of the quest for identity) become the context of the debate over authenticity, convention, and innovation in artistic expression.

Wilson Harris alludes to the inherent duality of the legend of El Dorado (which he refers to as an "open myth") and its relevance to the creative process in the following comment:

> The religious and economic thirst for exploration was true of the Spanish conquistador, of the Portuguese, French, Dutch and English, of Raleigh, of Fawcett, as it is true of the black modern pork-knocker and pork-knocker of all races. An instinctive idealism associated with this adventure was overpowered within individual and collective by enormous greed, cruelty and exploitation. In fact it would have been very difficult a century ago to present these exploits as other than a very material and degrading hunger for wealth spiced by a kind of self-

righteous spirituality. It is difficult enough today within clouds of prejudice and nihilism; nevertheless the substance of this adventure, involving men of all races, past and present conditions, has begun to acquire a residual pattern of illuminating correspondences. El Dorado, City of Gold, City of God, grotesque, unique coincidence, another window upon the Universe, another drunken boat, another ocean, another river; in terms of the novel the distribution of a frail moment of illuminating adjustments within a long succession and grotesque series of adventures, past and present, capable *now* of discovering themselves and continuing to discover themselves so that in one sense one relives and reverses the "given" conditions of the past, freeing oneself from catastrophic idolatry and blindness to one's own historical and philosophical conceptions and misconceptions which may bind one within a statuesque present or a false future.[13]

As Hena Maes-Jelinek points out the legend of El Dorado is frequently associated with the notion of creation.[14] This relationship, however, is not limited to the creation of empire but includes the original sense of creation of the world (Genesis) and the creation of the word. The legend of El Dorado with its characteristic features of duality, transformation, and creation suggests the alchemical process that is the central metaphor in the mythopoeic structure of both *The Lost Steps* and *Palace of the Peacock*.

An aura of apocalypse dominates the opening pages of the two novels, where the fictional world, whether located in the savannahs of Guyana as in *Palace* or the streets of a modern North American city as in *Lost Steps,* is portrayed as a prison and "battleground of the spirit." The alienation of the protagonists of the two novels is given different configurations, but both are fated to undertake a journey that becomes the retracing of lost steps on a historical and personal level.

In *Palace of the Peacock* the reader is immediately plunged into the hallucinatory world of the subconscious imagination. Time, place, character, and event are caught up in the flux of duality and metamorphosis. Whereas Carpentier's novel is firmly anchored in concrete reality, in *Palace* the objective world of historical or chronological time is barely recognizable. Through the language of the text itself, Harris achieves a fusion of past, present, and future, the simultaneity of dreamtime. As in the other novels of the Guiana Quartet, the primary reference is not the outer world but the subjective inner world.

Thus *Palace* opens with the narrator's prophetic dream about a horseman galloping along an open savannah road who is suddenly shot as if from nowhere. The horseman is his brother Donne, a modern counterpart of the European adventurer and conqueror, who exploits the indigenous population of Guyana in order to cultivate his rice and cattle estate.[15] Because of Donne's cruelty, his Amerindian work force has fled into the jungle.

Donne sees himself as the all-powerful sovereign of the savannahs. He arrogantly boasts: "Life here is tough. One has to be a devil to survive. I'm the last landlord. I tell you I fight everything in nature, flood, drought, chicken hawk, rat, beast, and woman. I'm everything. Midwife, yes, doctor, yes, gaoler, judge, hangman, every blasted thing to the labouring people" (*Palace* 17). Assuming the role of conqueror and colonizer, his motto is "Rule the land . . . And you rule the world" (*Palace* 19). He rationalizes his harsh treatment of the Amerindian folk in the name of "balance and perspective," since he considers them primitive, untrustworthy, and irresponsible and their flight a deliberate attempt to thwart his "right" to exploit the land.

Yet, as brutal and contemptuous as Donne is toward the Amerindians, Harris does not cast him in a rigid mold. The narrator, for example, recognizes Donne as the other half of his divided self: "I felt my heart come into my mouth with a sense of recognition and fear. Apart from this fleeting wishful resemblance it suddenly seemed to me I had never known Donne in the past—his face was a dead blank. I saw him now for the first faceless time as the captain and unnatural soul of heaven's dream; he was myself standing outside of me while I stood inside of him" (*Palace* 23). Donne and his brother, the Dreamer, are split-off fragments of each other's personality, representing the outer material self and the inner spiritual self. Furthermore, as Michael Gilkes suggests, they are like "the brothers of Greek mythology, Thanatos ('dead' historical time) and Hypnos ('living' mythological time)."[16] This interpretation of the relationship between Donne and the Dreamer fits Harris's concept of history as "a static clock that crushes all into the time of the conquest,"[17] as opposed to the liberating effect of the "intuitive logic" associated with myth and the subconscious. In *Palace* the erosion of absolute categories of reality applies to the representation of character as well as the "facts" of history.

The principle of duality, seen in the contrasting figures of the two brothers, is extended to all levels of the narrative. Donne's alienation is estrangement from self as well as estrangement from those he seeks to rule. In his brother's dream he is ambushed and killed by his Amerindian mistress Mariella, who is referred to as his muse and phantom, his victim and executioner. Mariella bears the name of the mission above the falls in the rain forest where her people have fled. The Dreamer identifies her with the lost innocence of Donne's first journey into the interior and the "immortal chase of love" (*Palace* 31). Mariella therefore represents, like the legend of El Dorado, the latent capacity for fulfillment in Donne's pursuit of the Amerindians.[18]

In contrast to the seemingly barren, isolated savannahs of Donne's would-be "kingdom and republic," emptied of the particulars of time and place, the opening pages of *Lost Steps* is set in the urban labyrinth of a modern metropolis. The city is a concrete jungle where seasons "leave no memory." Unlike *Palace*, the juxtaposition of Thanatos and Hypnos in *Lost Steps* is not based on the direct representation of a hallucinatory dream world. The disorientation in space and time presented in the first pages of the novel stem from the narrator-protagonist's sense of being trapped in a dead present, as the epigraph from Deuteronomy suggests. He is a contemporary Sisyphus, condemned to live in a claustrophobic, oppressive world:

> There were gaps of weeks in the chronicle of my existence, seasons that left with me no real memory, no unusual sensation, no enduring emotion; days when every gesture left me with the obsession that I had done the same thing before under identical circumstances—that I had been sitting in the same corner, that I had been telling the same story, looking at the schooner imprisoned in the glass of a paperweight. . . . Ascending and descending the hill of days, with the same stone on my back, I kept going through a momentum acquired in jerks and spasms. (*Lost Steps* 19–20)

He lives a modern life of anonymity, bearing the weight of historical time, which marks a steady rhythm of decay. In this age of paradise lost, he is even deprived of the heroism of selling his soul to the devil; he is instead a slave to the Bookkeeper and the Galley Master. Whereas in *Palace* the theme of alienation is given an archetypal significance (the divided self as the human condition in all ages), the alienation of the protagonist of *Lost Steps* is presented as the immediate result of a civilization ruled by technology and the demands of a consumer society.

Furthermore, the protagonist of Carpentier's autobiographical novel is a Latin American artist-intellectual cut off from his cultural roots and the ideals of his youth. Like Donne, Carpentier's protagonist has a double, but he is conscious that his alter ego resides within himself as judge of his unfulfilled aspirations: "Between the I that was and the I that I might have been the dark abyss of the lost years gaped. We lived together in one body, he and I, upheld by a secret architecture that was already—in our life, in our flesh—the presence of our death" (*Lost Steps* 30). Where the ruthless Donne sees himself as the captain of his own destiny, the protagonist of *Lost Steps* sees himself as the pawn of historical circumstance. He left his native country at an early age for North America with his European father, who indoctrinated him with the idea that the so-called New World was "a hemisphere without history, alien to the great Mediterranean traditions, a land of Indians and Negroes peopled by the offscourings of the great nations of Europe" (*Lost Steps* 83). Contrary to his father's teachings, when the protagonist arrives in Europe on the eve of World War II, instead of finding common laborers listening to Beethoven's Ninth Symphony, he witnesses the parade of young "philosophers" goose-stepping to the tune of Fascism. Bitterly disillusioned by the European "Dance of Death," he loses all faith in humanity and the power of "great" art.

After the war, he returns to the North American city of his adolescence, where he drifts into the drudgery of a routine existence writing musical scores for commercial films, "chained to [his] technique among clocks, chronographs, and metronomes in windowless, artificially lighted rooms lined with felt and soundproofed" (*Lost Steps*

20). The specter of Goya's *Cronos* dominates his daily life. Bored with his marriage, friends, and work, he expresses nostalgia for a lost sense of unity when he wonders whether in the past other men had longed for certain ways of living that had disappeared forever.

A chance encounter with a former teacher, the elderly curator of a museum of organography, offers Carpentier's protagonist an opportunity to escape his routine existence. This father figure reminds him of his past work as a musicologist investigating the origins of primitive music. Reluctantly, the protagonist agrees to go on an expedition in the jungles of Venezuela in search of primitive instruments for the museum collection. The journey toward self in both *Lost Steps* and *Palace* thus involves a return to the aboriginal past, the creative reestablishment of the "first time" of Genesis in the privileged space of the rain forest.

In the initial stages of the journey in both novels, the protagonists arrive at a real and symbolic place where they begin to let go of their "death-in-life" existence: the Mission of Mariella in *Palace* and the anonymous South American capital in *Lost Steps*. For the protagonist of Carpentier's novel, the sights, sounds, and smells of the tropical city begin to awaken memories of his forgotten past. At first he regrets having undertaken the trip and feels uncomfortable away from his familiar though alienating environment. His journey, however, is a dual process of separation and return, which he immediately experiences as a reencounter with the language of his childhood: "A strange voluptuousness was lulling my scruples. And a force was slowly invading me through my ears, my pores: the language. Here once more was the language I had talked in my infancy; the language in which I had learned to read and sol-fa; the language that had grown rusty with disuse, thrown aside like a useless instrument in a country where it was of no value to me" (*Lost Steps* 45).

Within the mythopoeic structure of *Lost Steps*, memory is linked to the recovery of original language. Memory and language as manifestations of psychic awareness are therefore emphasized throughout the first stages of the journey. Beginning with the protagonist's arrival in his native country, written language is given special significance, since the unfolding of consciousness is presented in the form of journal entries. Furthermore, since language is associated with the verbal expression of cultural identity, Carpentier uses the first stages of the journey to contrast, as he does in so much of his writing, the decadence of European civilization with the vitality of the Americas.

The conflict between European and American culture is outwardly represented by the two women Mouche and Rosario. Mouche, the protagonist's French mistress who accompanies him on the trip, is a cosmopolitan pseudo-intellectual who begins to deteriorate in the natural environment of the tropics. On the other hand, the Indian woman Rosario is described as "a living sum of the races," a woman of the land who lives in a perpetual present in easy communion with nature. When the protagonist reaches the next stage of his journey, he will abandon Mouche and take up a new life with Rosario, symbolically leaving behind the existential burden of history and the alienation of modern European civilization for a simpler, more spontaneous life outside of chronological time.

In the same way that memory breaks through the surface of the protagonist's consciousness to uncover original language, the nearby jungle threatens to reclaim the urban landscape of the South American capital. Roots of tropical vegetation push up through cracks in sidewalks and buildings, undermining the city's facade of modernity and progress:

> Something like a baleful pollen in the air—a ghost pollen, impalpable rot, enveloping decay—suddenly became active with mysterious design, opening what was closed, closing what was open, upsetting calculations, contradicting specific gravity, making guarantees worthless. One morning the ampoules of serum in a hospital were found to be full of mole; precision instruments were not registering correctly; certain liquors began to bubble in the bottle; the Rubens National Museum was attacked by an unknown parasite immune to sprays. (*Lost Steps* 43–44).

The local explanation for nature's defiance of civilization is the theory of the Worm, the return of the repressed: "Nobody had ever seen the Worm. But the Worm existed, carrying on its arts of confusion, turning up when least expected to confound the most tried and trusted experience" (*Lost Steps* 44).

When a revolution breaks out shortly after his arrival, the protagonist is just as mystified about the cause of the political violence as the foreigners in his hotel who bemoan the fate of these *mestizo* countries always on the verge of chaos. But he recognizes the conflict between the conservatives and radicals as a "chronological discrepancy of ideals," as if the warring sides were living in different centuries or, as a local lawyer puts it, within the tradition of a people accustomed to living with the conflicting ideals of Rousseau, the Inquisition, the Immaculate Conception, and *Das Kapital* (*Lost Steps* 53).

Despite the political upheaval, the protagonist's return to his native country has a salutary effect on his mind and spirit. For the first time in years, he is able to sleep through the night without the aid of eye mask or drugs. But the renewed contact with the world of his childhood also leads to a sense of distance from his French mistress, who seems bored and unable to respond spontaneously to the new environment. He begins to see her as a burden associated with the life he had hoped to escape.

It is during a short trip outside the capital in the provincial town of Los Altos that he begins to understand the true source of his alienation. He meets three young artists—a black painter, an Indian poet, and a white musician—whom he disdainfully refers to as the Three Magi because of their eager attention to his mistress, who enthralls them with anecdotes about Paris and the latest developments in the European avant-garde. Infuriated by their reverence for European culture and their total indifference to the history and traditions of their own country, he recognizes in these young men the false direction of his own youth:

> That night as I looked at them I could see the harm my uprooting from this environment, which had been mine until adolescence, had done me; the share the facile bedazzlement of the members of my generation, carried away by theories into the same intellectual labyrinths, devoured by the same Minotaurs, had had in disorienting me. I was weary of dragging the chain of certain ideas, and I felt a lurking desire to say something that was not the daily cliché of all who considered themselves *au courant* with things that fifteen years from now would be contemptuously cast aside. (*Lost Steps* 71)

At one time these discussions had amused him, but here in the natural environment of the tropics, he finds this empty talk of European theories of art unbearable. The contrast between the local folk art and the "false mysteries" of the European avant-garde awakens in him a renewed sense of purpose and direction. His stay in the capital and Los Altos puts him in touch with his earliest memories, the period from childhood to adolescence before his condition of cultural exile, and prepares him for the journey beyond Los Altos into the interior.

This journey is divided into four major episodes in which Carpentier establishes a metaphorical relationship between landscape and history: La Sierra, El Valle de las Llamas, las Tierras del Caballo, and las Tierras del Perro. At each of these places, the protagonist meets a member of the crew that will accompany him on the journey to the interior: the Indian woman Rosario, the diamond hunter Yannes, the missionary Fray Pedro de Henostras, the adventurer El Adelantado, and finally the herbalist and storyteller who perpetuates the legend of El Dorado, Montsalvatje.[19] On a historical level these figures are associated with the European conquest. Rosario, however, is linked to the pre-Columbian past and New World cultural synthesis.

Carpentier's protagonist travels first by bus over the Andes and then by riverboat through colonial towns, remote villages, and primitive settlements along the banks of the Orinoco. He observes that the simultaneity of past, present, and future time is not mere poetic fantasy in South America but an actual experience of everyday life:

> The years are subtracted, melt away, vanish, in the dizzying backward flight of time. We have not yet come to the sixteenth century. It is much earlier. We are in the Middle Ages. For it is not the man of the Renaissance who carried out the Discovery and the Conquest, but medieval man. . . . When behold, this past had suddenly become the present. I could touch and breathe it. I now saw the breathtaking possibility of traveling in time, as others travel in space. (*Lost Steps* 57–58)

The protagonist's journey is thus a voyage backward through the historical stages of human development to the beginning of time, but it is above all a flight from the modern world toward nature.[20] The principal figure in *Lost Steps* associated with nature is Rosario. The protagonist first encounters her on a mountain road on the bus trip beyond Los Altos. He soon recognizes this *mujer de la tierra* as a medium through whom "plants began to speak and describe their own powers" (*Lost Steps* 80).

As the protagonist and his companions get closer to the boundaries of the rain forest, he feels more drawn to Rosario, and more distant toward his mistress Mouche, who seems increasingly alien, incapable of establishing any relationship between herself and her surroundings. Together Mouche and Rosario, like Mariella in *Palace*, represent the dual aspects of the protagonist's unconscious. They are contrasting images of the spiritual death of the artificial world he has left behind and the regenerative powers of the natural world he is about to enter. While Mouche is the personification of the separation between nature and culture characteristic of modernity, Rosario represents the connection to a lost sense of unity, the fusion of history and nature.[21]

Before the protagonist can be initiated into the "marvelous" realm of the rain forest, he must relinquish his ties with Mouche.[22] The forces of nature aid him in achieving this separation. Mouche violates the moral code of her new environment when she makes sexual advances toward Rosario. Outraged by this offense, Rosario pummels her with a stick, literally shattering the French woman's mask of modernity. Mouche is then stricken with malaria, a final defeat that the protagonist sees as "*un ejemplar desquite de lo cabal y lo auténtico*"—the perfect revenge of the authentic on the false (*Lost Steps* 134). Since it is obvious that Mouche is not fit for the adventure that awaits the protagonist, the herbalist Montsalvatje volunteers to take her back downriver where she can regain her health in comfort. The protagonist is now free to continue his journey with Rosario and the other members of the crew.

While the symbolism of the fictional characters in *Lost Steps* is obvious, the characters in *Palace* are more elusive since they are presented in the narrative as a montage of shifting images and perspectives. Likewise, compared to *Lost Steps*, the narrative structure of *Palace* seems diffuse and random. Rather than plot as such, the novel develops in a series of psychic illuminations.[23] As we saw in the *The*

74

Secret Ladder, Harris conceives of his characters as "agents of person-ality" rather than representations of individual consciousness.[24]

The only thing we know for certain about the characters in *Palace* is that they have joined the violent taskmaster Donne in the pursuit of his rebellious Amerindian laborers. Bits and pieces of their racial and social background are revealed in the course of the journey more as a means of showing how they are all bound together in the same "repetitive boat and prison of life" than to highlight the individual differences among them. They are motivated by inexplicable presen-timents and a nebulous desire for personal fulfillment that operates on a primarily subconscious level.

When Donne and his crew arrive at the Mission of Mariella in their guise as modern-day conquistadors, the Amerindians quickly flee from their homes into the surrounding jungle. The atmosphere of the abandoned settlement exerts a strange power over the racially mixed crew, who are all escapees from modern civilization seeking refuge in the bush from their personal failures. In the hallucinatory landscape of the rain forest, they begin to unearth the "grave of memory," reflecting on the frustrations and lack of fulfillment in their past lives. We learn, for example, that Cameron, the great-grandson of a Scot-tish adventurer and an African slave, has spent his life searching for "space and freedom to use his own hands in order to make his own primitive home and kingdom on earth" (*Palace* 42).

In the depths of the rain forest even Donne begins to shed his mask of stoicism and cruelty. He admits to treating the Amerindians harshly and expresses a desire to establish a different relationship with them. Ultimately, however, he decides to act in his own inter-est—to continue the pursuit and to force them back to his land. When he returns to camp one morning, accompanied by an old Arawak woman he has taken prisoner, his brother the Dreamer has an intuition of tragedy, which he describes as "an undigested morsel of recollection [that] erased all present waking sensation and evoked a future time, petrifying and painful, confused and unjust" (*Palace* 54). This "memory" of the future is experienced by the other mem-bers of the crew as well;[25] they all feel drawn together in their "inverse craft" toward some new beginning. We discover that they all bear the names of a famous crew that had drowned on a similar expedition. The journey to Mariella will lead them to their second death, which becomes their spiritual rebirth.

When Donne and his crew set off again in search of the folk, they take the old Arawak woman as their guide. Her presence recalls the history of the conquest, but since Harris rejects any interpretation of history that consolidates the victor/victim conflict, she is portrayed as the "ancestral embroidery and obsession" of the crew, the longing for fulfillment of all races of men in all ages:

> Her race was a vanishing one overpowered by the fantasy of a Catholic as well as a Protestant invasion. This cross she had forgotten in an earlier dream of distant centuries and a returning to the Siberian unconscious pilgrimage in the straits where life had possessed and abandoned at the same time the apprehension of a facile beginning and ending. An unearthly pointlessness was her true manner, and an all-inclusive manner that still contrived to be—as a duck sheds water from its wings—the negation of every threat of conquest and fear—every shade of persecution wherein was drawn and mingled the pursued and the pursuer alike, separate and yet one and the same person. (*Palace* 72)

As Donne and his men struggle against hazardous river rapids, the disturbing presence of the old woman seems to merge with the churning waters, luring them to their deaths:

> The sudden dreaming fury of the stream was naught else but the ancient spit of all flying insolence in the voiceless and terrible humility of the folk. Tiny embroideries resembling the handwork of the Arawak woman's kerchief and the wrinkles on her brow turned to incredible and fast soundless breakers of foam. Her crumpled bosom and river grew agitated with desire, bottling and shaking every fear and inhibition and outcry. The ruffles in the water were her dress rolling and rising to embrace the crew. This sudden insolence of soul rose and caught them from the powder of her eyes and the age of her smile and the dust in her hair all flowing back upon them with silent streaming majesty and abnormal youth and in a wave of freedom and strength. (*Palace* 73)

Hena Maes-Jelinek interprets the youthful transformation of the old Arawak woman as the symbolic reincarnation of Donne's muse and executioner, Mariella.[26] In her role as spiritual guide and primordial mother, similar to that of the Indian woman Rosario in *Lost Steps*, she leads the crew through the "straits of memory" toward a renewal of consciousness:

> The crew were transformed by the awesome spectacle of a voiceless soundless motion, the purest appearance of vision in the chaos of emotional sense. Earthquake and volcanic water appeared to seize them and stop their ears dashing the scales only from their eyes. They saw the naked unequivocal flowing peril and beauty and soul of the pursuer and the pursued all together, and they knew they would perish if they dreamed to turn back. (*Palace* 73)

This descent into the "complex womb" of history and nature signals the beginning of the trials of initiation of the final stage of the journey, which takes seven days—a paradoxical reversal of the seven days of Creation during which time each crew member meets his death.[27] The first to lose his life in the raging river rapids is Carroll, the youngest member of the crew. We learn of old Schomburgh's guilt-ridden relationship to Carroll, who is both his son and nephew. In his youth Schomburgh had fallen in love with Carroll's mother; he later discovered that she was his half-sister. The young woman married another man while Carroll was still an infant but refused to give her son the husband's name. The illegitimacy, incest, and racial *mestizaje* that characterize Carroll's family history are symbolic of Guyanese social history: "Who and what was Carroll? Schomburgh had glimpsed . . . the embodiment of hate and love, the ambiguity of everyone and no-one. He had recognized his true son, nameless out of shame and yet named with a new distant name by a muse and a mother to make others equally nameless out of mythical shame and a name, and to forge for their descendants new mythical farflung relationships out of their nameless shame and fear" (*Palace* 83).

Carroll's condition of namelessness indicates the role of origins and cultural identity in the quest. Donne's name is thought to possess "a cruel glory," the emblem of power and command. The young Carroll's death, however, is a baptism in the nameless community of spirit that transcends "every material mask and label and economic form"—the ultimate object of the quest. As the riverboat forges

77

ahead toward the waterfalls above the Mission of Mariella and each successive crew member dies, it is in their "second death" that they overcome their inner conflicts, achieving self-knowledge and spiritual wholeness:

> Now [Donne] knew for the first time the fetishes he and his companions embraced. They were bound together in wishful substance and in the very enormity of a dreaming enmity and opposition and self-destruction. Remove all this or weaken its appearance and its cruelty and they were finished. So Donne had died in the death of Wishrop; Jenning's primitive abstraction and slackening will was a reflection of the death of Cameron; Schomburgh had died with Carroll. And da Silva saw with dread his own sogging fool's life on the threshold of the ultimate stab of discredit like one who had adventured and lived on scraps of vulgar intention and detection and rumour that passed for the arrest of spiritual myth and the rediscovery of a new life in the folk. (*Palace* 123)

Donne and the other members of the crew—all aspects of a fragmented psyche—are reunited in the apotheosis of the seventh day of their journey beyond Mariella. Freed from their worldly illusions, one by one they climb up the ladders of a radiant waterfall until they reach the "Palace of the Peacock," the City of Gold, where all principles of opposition cease. The narrating I, now speaking as one for Donne and the Dreamer, merges in ecstatic harmony with the universe:

> One was what I am in the music—buoyed and supported above dreams by the undivided soul and anima in the universe from whom the word of dance and recreation first came, the command to the starred peacock who was instantly transported to know and to hug to himself his true invisible otherness and opposition, his true alien spiritual love without cruelty and confusion in the blindness and frustration of desire. It was the dance of all fulfillment I now held and knew deeply, cancelling my forgotten fear of strangeness and catastrophe in a destitute world. (*Palace* 152)

The protagonist transcends the finite existence of historical time and enters a timeless mystical sphere.[28] The search for the primitive folk in *Palace of the Peacock* thus becomes a search for the mythical paradise of union with the cosmos—a timeless place of supreme liberation.

In *Lost Steps* the protagonist is allowed no such mystical transcendence. Determined to overcome the cultural barrier that separates him from Rosario and the indigenous people of the interior, he undertakes the final stage of his river journey into the "alchemical laboratory" of the rain forest: "Everything here seemed something else, thus creating a world of appearances that concealed reality, casting doubt on many truths. . . . The jungle is the world of deceit, subterfuge, duplicity; everything there is disguise, stratagem, artifice, metamorphosis" (*Lost Steps* 147).

As the protagonist and his companions break away from the banks of civilization and historical time, the river seems to lead them back to the mythical time of Genesis. First, however, they must pass through treacherous river rapids, evoking—as in *Palace of the Peacock*—the trials of Ulysses' crew. Fearing for his life, the protagonist clings to Rosario who seems surprisingly calm and unafraid. They finally reach Santa Monica de los Venados in "The Valley Where Time Had Stopped," a primitive settlement forged out of the adventurer El Adelantado's desire for a "kingdom on earth." Reminiscent of Cameron in *Palace*, El Adelantado explains how he gave up his search for gold and founded Santa Monica because he was now "much more interested in the land and in the power of decreeing its laws" (*Lost Steps* 170).

Upon taking up his new life with Rosario in Santa Monica, the protagonist loses all sense of chronological time and becomes *un hombre físico*, a natural man, who learns to walk to the rhythm of the universe. Little cracks, however, begin to appear in his vision of an earthly paradise. Santa Monica is neither the Garden of Eden nor Manoa, the City of Gold. He finds that as El Adelantado had warned him, "Creation is no laughing matter" (*Lost Steps* 171).

There are times of disease and hunger, and even moments of brutality and violence. For example, when a leper violates one of the children of the settlement, the inhabitants demand his death. El Adelantado's son Marcos takes the protagonist with him in search of the offender. But when they find him, the protagonist cannot assume the role of executioner. He realizes that from the moment he pulled the trigger, "*something would be changed forever.* There are some acts that throw up walls, markers, limits in a man's existence" (*Lost Steps* 200). This confrontation with the harsh reality of historical circumstance anticipates the conclusion of the protagonist's adventure in The Valley Where Time Had Stopped.[29]

During a long and boring rainy period, the protagonist is overcome with a desire to write music. Far away from concert halls and artistic controversies, his sojourn in paradise has unlocked his creative powers, but he lacks the simplest tools to make use of them, such as pen and paper. Moreover, he realizes that art must have an audience and thus belongs to the world he has left behind.

While he is struggling to come to terms with this new kind of frustration, a search plane lands in the jungle clearing. When he learns that the men in the plane have been sent by his wife to rescue him from some imagined danger, he feels compelled to return to civilization if only to settle his personal affairs and obtain the materials he needs to carry out his work. Like the men of Ulysses' crew in the land of the lotus eaters, he is snatched from his mythical paradise.

Although he is determined to return, he finds that it is impossible to repeat the miracle, to "*desandar lo andado.*" When he tries to get back to Santa Monica six months later, he is unable to locate the narrow jungle passage that leads to El Adelantado's settlement because the river is too high. Moreover, he discovers that Rosario has taken up with another man. His hope of regaining his mythical existence is lost forever. Finally, he realizes that as an artist, unlike Rosario and the indigenous people of Santa Monica, he cannot escape history, "because the only human race to which it is forbidden to sever the bonds of time is the race of those who create art, and who not only must move ahead of the immediate yesterday, represented by tangible witness, but must anticipate the song and the form of others who will follow them, creating new tangible witness with full awareness of what has been done up to the moment" (*Lost Steps* 238–39).

Where in *Palace of the Peacock* Wilson Harris sees myth and its variable art as a means of reversing the "given conditions of the past," in *Lost Steps* Carpentier concludes that history is inescapable. As a point of departure, both Harris and Carpentier use myth as a means of refuting the notion of a historyless, cultureless Caribbean and Latin America, but for Harris myth or the mythic imagination is tantamount to deliverance from the alienating effects of the historical process. In *Lost Steps*, however, Carpentier suggests the abolition of historical time and participation in mythic time as an alternative to the Sisyphus syndrome of modern life, only to deny this as a real possibility at the end of the novel.

According to Roberto González Echevarría, the protagonist's journey in *Lost Steps* is a "failed quest" since he is unable either to complete his musical score in Santa Monica or to establish a lasting relationship with Rosario. Echevarría thus concludes that "there is no genesis in the novel, only repetitions, rediscoveries and falsifications."[30] There is indeed a process of demystification at work in *Lost Steps;* the protagonist must give up his romantic notions of an earthly paradise. There is also, however, a *genesis* of consciousness; at the end of the journey, the protagonist understands the nature of his alienation in a cultural sense as well as in broader existential terms. Furthermore, he arrives at an important understanding of the creative process. For as Harry Slochower points out, the mythopoeic work precludes the possibility of absolute transcendence; the quest "is not eliminated but assimilated."[31]

In *The Lost Steps* and *Palace of the Peacock* Carpentier and Harris pose similar questions about art and the creative process. It is in the creative space of the Venezuelan rain forest that the protagonist of *Lost Steps* revises his theory of the origin of music as the imitation of nature; his experience with the indigenous people of the interior convinces him that music originated in magic. Although Carpentier concludes that the modern writer cannot regain the mythical El Dorado where "history and fable are one," like Harris he believes that the novelist must go beyond a mere imitation of reality toward a creative, magical conception of art as symbolic form.

PART THREE

Myth and History:
The Dialectics
of Culture

CHAPTER 4

History as Mythic Discourse:
El siglo de las luces,
Tumatumari, and
La case du commandeur

T he problematic nature of the quest for origins posed in Carpentier's *Los pasos perdidos* and Harris's *Palace of the Peacock* lead both writers to a reinterpretation of the quest in later novels, such as *El siglo de las luces* (1962) and *Tumatumari* (1968). In both of these novels as well as Glissant's *La case du commandeur* (The overseer's hut, 1981), the quest takes place within the conceptual framework of a dialectical relationship between myth and history. The principal metaphor that expresses this relationship in the three texts is the spiral—the spatial configuration of the conch shell in *El siglo,* the whirlpool in *Tumatumari,* and the temporal vortex in *La case.* In each of these novels, there is a merging of family and social history in which a woman plays a central role in the development of the narrative. The female protagonists function as mediators between conflicting forces in Caribbean history and culture. These women represent alternative approaches to the concept of history questioned in the earlier novels and different ways of participating in the historical process.

In his study of Carpentier's fiction, Roberto González Echevarría considers *El siglo de las luces* a "revision" of the Cuban writer's literary tenets of the forties. He sees works such as *El reino de este mundo* as an attempt to express a "complicity between nature, history and the narrative process" based on the philosophical premises of Oswald Spengler. In this regard, Carpentier is said to have assumed the Spenglerian model of history—a circular pattern of endless repetitions based on the cycles of nature; furthermore, the fusion of nature and history in works such as *El reino* is seen as an expression of Carpentier's desire to show a natural link between landscape (*terra mater*) and the creative process.[1] These ideas are then challenged in *Los pasos perdidos* when the narrator-protagonist fails to reintegrate himself into the indigenous culture of the Americas, and they are finally superseded altogether in the dialectical framework of *El siglo de las luces*.

Although Spengler undoubtedly played a key role in Carpentier's conception of the narrative process in his earlier fiction, I believe González Echevarría overemphasizes the Spengler influence. As we saw in the analysis of *El reino*, the depersonalized, ironic structure of the novel does underscore the problematic nature of the author's concept of the marvelous as unmediated revelation of the "primal essence" of Latin American and Caribbean reality.[2] Nevertheless, *El reino* does not present Spengler's static vision of history since the cyclical structure of the narrative is not the perfect circle of the cosmogonic round but reveals elements of transformation and progress. Despite the repeated series of betrayals and disillusionment, slavery and colonialism are abolished. Furthermore, the source of the slave rebellions in *El reino* is not nature but the desire for freedom, and as the conclusion of the novel indicates each failure to achieve true freedom will lead to a renewed quest, which neither results in total fulfillment nor total regression. The concept of a dialectical movement of history that González Echevarría sees in the later novel *El siglo de las luces* is therefore already suggested in *El reino*.[3]

Furthermore, Echevarría does not take into account the transformative role of myth implicit in the archetypal structure of the quest in both *El reino* and *Los pasos*. Neither the author himself in *El reino* nor the narrator-protagonist of *Los pasos* can reestablish the harmonious relationship between nature and culture presumably characteristic of the autochthonous African and Amerindian traditions. Their quest, however, leads to a new understanding of the relationship between myth and history. For as Labanyi points out in his discussion of *Los pasos*, "Man's integration into history cannot take the form of the return to some primary origin, for History (to use Sartre's terminology) has, like man, no essence but only existence. History, like Art, consists of a constant process of transformation."[4] If art is viewed as a corollary of the mythic imagination, we can understand how the myths of the African gods that inspired the slave revolts in *El reino* and the Amerindian myth of El Dorado in *Los pasos* are transformed into the revolutionary myth of the promised land in *El siglo*, a secular myth of liberation oriented toward the future rather than the past.[5]

The historical context of *El siglo* is the Caribbean and Europe during the period of the French Revolution from 1789 to 1809. In this respect, Carpentier's later novel coincides with the historical themes of *El reino*. *El siglo*, however, offers a panoramic view of the whole Caribbean, including the Guianas and Venezuela, indicating in this way the common historical roots of the area. The narrative begins in Havana on the eve of the Haitian slave rebellion against the French colonists. This revealing study of revolution and the cataclysmic effects of history is related from the perspective of the children of an upper-class family who reject the social values of the creole aristocracy in Cuba.[6]

As in *El reino*, Carpentier turns to the issue of how the doctrines of the Enlightenment "illuminated" the Americas. Influenced by the abstract ideals of the Declaration of the Rights of Man, the young protagonists of *El siglo* must confront the contradictions of historical reality: the dogmatism, political cynicism, and greed for personal power that betray the spirit of the Revolution. The Enlightenment is doubly important in *El siglo* because of its historical impact on the nineteenth-century struggles for independence in the Americas and its role in promoting the secular view of human endeavors that marked the emergence of modern times. Much of the philosophical debate in the novel centers on the separation of spiritual and secular beliefs, intuition and reason, heart and mind.

El siglo de las luces opens in Havana at the home of a wealthy Cuban merchant who has just died, leaving an orphaned son and daughter, Carlos and Sofia, and a nephew, Esteban. The three adolescents spend their first year of mourning sheltered from the outside world. In the absence of paternal authority, they are free to pass the time as they wish, eating and sleeping at odd hours, and transforming the family mansion into a house of "perpetual games." Their home, now a disorderly labyrinth of unpacked shipping crates, becomes the privileged space of childhood fantasies. Their harmonious existence in the midst of external chaos is brought to an abrupt end, however, when a stranger arrives looking for their father on a stormy Easter Sunday.

The sudden intrusion of Victor Hugues, a cosmopolitan businessman from Port-au-Prince, sets in motion the process that will transform the lives of the adolescents. He restores order to the house and assumes the role of surrogate father; and as such Victor replaces the old values associated with the deceased father and introduces both Esteban and Sofia into the world of adulthood. Most important, he introduces the Cuban adolescents to the liberal ideas of the Enlightenment and the French Revolution. When Victor, a freemason, is threatened with arrest by the colonial authorities because of his subversive ideas, Sofia offers the family finca as a refuge for him and his friend Ogé, a mulatto doctor from Saint Domingue. She and Esteban accompany the two men to the country estate where they are fascinated by heated political discussions about revolution, class war, liberty, and equality:

> They talked of nothing but revolutions, and Sofia was amazed at the passions which this new topic of conversation aroused. To talk revolutions, to imagine revolutions, to place oneself mentally in the midst of a revolution, is in some small degree to become master of the world. Those who talk of revolutions find themselves driven to making them. It is so obvious that such and such a privilege must be abolished that they proceed to abolish it; it is so true that such and such an oppression is detestable that measures are concerted against it; it is so apparent that such and such a person is a villain that he is unanimously condemned to death. Then, once the ground has been cleared, they proceed to build the City of the Future.[7]

Although Victor and Ogé seem to use the same language in their discussions about the necessity for social change, Esteban suspects that there is some important difference in the way they view the nature of human progress. While Victor upholds the egalitarian principles of the Declaration of the Rights of Man, he is primarily concerned with business; for him the "advanced ideas" of the New Age are important because they challenge the colonial monopoly of trade in the Americas. He is one of several creole merchants who has set up a contraband organization to circumvent the Spanish monopoly in particular. His mission in Havana was to contact local merchants sympathetic to freemasonry in order to form a secret organization to combat the economic tyranny of Spain, but he found little active interest in social issues among the Cubans whom he describes as "people [who] seemed to be asleep, inert, living in a timeless marginal world, suspended between tobacco and sugar" (69).

While Victor has no use for religion and metaphysics, Ogé believes the revolutionary process should involve more than just "snapping the chains" of the oppressed. Though a man of science, the Haitian mulatto espouses a form of revolutionary mysticism that aims to bring about change by awakening the transcendental powers of the human spirit. He disagrees with Victor's antireligious views and is of the opinion that "since man had always manifested a tenacious aspiration towards something that might be called 'imitation of Christ', this feeling should be transformed into a desire to go even further—to elevate himself into a sort of archetype of human perfection" (72).

Neither Sofia nor Esteban is interested in Ogé's notions of spiritual transcendence; they are more attracted to Victor's "scientific" views of human progress, and most of all his powerful presence as an energetic man of action. When Victor and Ogé are forced to escape the island, they invite Sofia and Esteban to accompany them on a trip to Port-au-Prince. During this unexpected sea voyage, Sofia yields to Victor's sexual advances and Esteban eagerly joins him in the revolutionary adventure that he hopes will be his initiation into manhood. Victor's relationship with Sofia and Esteban establishes the "triadic" structure upon which the rest of the narrative revolves.[8]

When their ship stops at Santiago de Cuba, the city is full of refugees from Saint Domingue; a slave uprising has swept across the northern part of the island forcing the white settlers to flee.[9] Victor leaves Sofia in the Cuban port and immediately proceeds to Port-au-Prince with Ogé and Esteban. On arriving, they find the city in flames and Victor's business establishment burned to the ground. But despite the destruction of his property, Victor feels a sense of freedom, a sense of being on the threshold of a new life: "His life was reduced to a cypher, without promises to fulfill, without debts to pay, suspended between a past which had been destroyed and a future it was impossible to foresee" (87).

Nevertheless, the uprising puts an end to his friendship with Ogé, whose younger brother has been executed by white settlers in Cap Français. The mulatto expresses bitterness toward all whites and warns Victor to leave before he is killed by the black insurgents.[10] The parting of the two friends anticipates the conflicts Victor will have to confront in his role as agent of the French Revolution in the Americas, especially as they relate to the issue of black emancipation and political expediency. Their separation marks the beginning of the "unimaginable" future in which Victor firmly establishes his materialist vision of historical and revolutionary change in opposition to the transcendental values associated with the Saint Domingue mulatto.

Victor, transformer of reality and "conjurer" of adventure in the lives of young Esteban and Sofia, is the figure associated with the principles of the Enlightenment. He is a bourgeois revolutionary who combines the efficiency of a tradesman with the ruthlessness of a Robespierre. As an energetic man of action who relies too heavily on a so-called scientific view of social change, he ultimately becomes a mere instrument of political expediency.

Esteban plunges into the tumult of history alongside Victor and sails toward his vision of the promised land in revolutionary France. In Paris Victor quickly aligns himself with the new government and begins his rise to power as Agent of the Revolution in the Americas. The major part of the novel deals with Esteban's initiation into the world of revolutionary politics and his disillusionment as he witnesses the degeneration of Victor's revolutionary claims.

It is through Esteban that Carpentier reintroduces the transcendental themes previously associated with Ogé. In the course of his journey with Victor, Esteban will lean more and more toward the "esoteric speculations" of the Haitian mulatto. Furthermore, Esteban fulfills Ogé's notion of life as an "imitation of Christ." Even at the beginning of the novel, the sickly, asthmatic young Esteban is identified with the Christ figure. Later he will recognize in the image of the crucifixion the meaning of his life as an adult: "Everything that could be said about Man and his World, all that might be contained in the notions of Light, Birth, and Darkness, was said—said for all eternity—in what passed between the stark geometry of the black wood and the fluid immensity of the universal womb, through that intermediary body at the crucial hour of his death and rebirth" (222). The symbolism of the cross as a dialogue between earth and water, the temporal and the eternal, characterizes Esteban's journey as a "miserable wanderer on a distant shore."

In Paris Esteban is caught up in the fervor of the French Revolution, but he is unable to keep pace with the dizzying shifts in revolutionary policy. No sooner than he internalizes one concept, the Revolution moves in a new direction:

> One seemed to be in the midst of a gigantic allegory of a revolution rather than a revolution itself, a metaphorical revolution, a revolution which had been made elsewhere, which revolved on a hidden axis, which had been elaborated in subterranean councils, invisible to those who wanted to know all about it. Esteban was unfamiliar with these new names, unknown yesterday and changing every day, and he could not discover who was responsible for the Revolution." (95)

When he is sent by Victor to work for the revolutionary cause in Bayonne on the Spanish frontier translating revolutionary literature for Spain, Esteban finds it even more difficult to understand the constantly changing political scene in Paris. Isolated in the remote Basque province, away from the excitement of the capital, he experiences the frustration of trying to transplant the spirit of the Revolution to a people who insist on preserving their own traditions. The Spanish émigrés are disgruntled with the policies of the French, and he feels that his own work as translator is boring and unimportant. Therefore when Esteban learns that Victor is leading a military expedition to Guadeloupe on behalf of the revolutionary government, he eagerly requests permission to join him.

Esteban leaves France still longing to take part in "Something Big" (118), but his reunion with Victor only leads to further disillusionment. Now an Agent of the Revolution, Victor returns to the New World with the guillotine and the Decree of the 16th Pluviose of the Year Two abolishing slavery in the French territories. The former baker and tradesman defeats the British in Guadeloupe, assumes governorship of the colony, and issues the proclamation of emancipation, but as Esteban observes, he is a changed man. Victor has become a cold, distant leader without friends who alienates his would-be supporters by his arrogance, arbitrary actions, and ruthless imposition of discipline and order.

When his idol Robespierre is executed by the government of the 9th Thermidor, Victor is outraged but manages to accommodate himself to every shift in revolutionary policy. He is now "a man who could do both good and evil with the same cold courage. He was as capable of being Ormuzd as he was of being Ahriman, of reigning over the kingdom of darkness as over the kingdom of light. According to what turn events were taking, he could suddenly turn into his own opposite" (322). The New World commissar inaugurates his own reign of terror in Guadeloupe, and Esteban witnesses the great conflagration that he once viewed as a necessary purification for the "birth of a new humanity" turn into an apocalyptic nightmare.

Esteban's only respite from Victor's Jacobin society in the Caribbean are his excursions into the countryside of Guadeloupe and a prolonged sailing expedition. He perceives his excursions into the natural world, away from the center of political turmoil, as an escape from history. Yet it is here in the lush tropical landscape of Basse-Terre and on the open sea that he encounters the natural signs that reveal the meaning of his own experience *in history*. Esteban's experience of climbing a tree is portrayed as a sensuous, mystical union with nature but it also suggests the transformative character of human endeavors:

After passing the first test, which meant reaching the inaccessible lower branches, he began to ascend toward the crown of the tree,

up a sort of spiral staircase of increasingly slender and more ser-
ried branches supporting the great cloak of foliage, the green beehive,
the sumptuous roof, which he was seeing from inside for the first
time. . . . As he climbed to his vantage-point, Esteban understood the
secret relationship so often established between the Mast, the Plough,
the Tree and the Cross. He remembered a text from Saint Hipploytus:
"This wood belongs to me. I nourish myself on it, I sustain myself with
it; I dwell in its roots, I rest in its branches; I give myself up to its
breathing as I give myself up to the wind. Here is my strait gate, here is
my narrow path; a Jacob's Ladder, at whose summit is the Lord." The
great symbols of Tau, the Cross of Saint Andrew, the Brazen Serpent,
the Anchor and the Ladder, were implicit in every tree; the Created
anticipated the Constructed, providing patterns for the future Builder
of the Arks. (161–62)

This symbolic act is an expression of Esteban's desire for a sense of
spiritual transcendence that has eluded him in the realm of social action. He intuitively understands the correspondence between the tree
as natural sign and numerous man-made symbols, such as the cross.
The common link in the series of emblems associated with the tree is
the suggestion of growth and transformation implicit in the natural
cycle of birth, death, and rebirth. The cross is particularly significant
in this respect since it combines the notions of sacrifice and redemp-
tion. What Esteban does not understand on a conscious level is the
relation between his desire for transcendence, what he later refers to
as the "ideal object of a future passion" (341), and his participation in
the historical process.

Esteban's ascent toward the crown of the tree is described as
movement up a spiral ladder. The spiral as emblem of the ascent of
history and consciousness is repeated in another instance when Esteban is ordered by Victor to leave Guadeloupe on a privateering
expedition. Since the ship engages in very few raids, Esteban is able
to immerse himself in the timelessness of life at sea, and during his
numerous explorations of isolated beaches he finds a total sense of
harmony, outside time and space. On one such occasion, naked and
alone, he contemplates a conch shell:

This snail was the mediator between evanescent, fugitive, lawless, mea-
sureless fluidity, and the land, with its crystallisations, its structures, its

morphology, where everything could be grasped and weighed. Out of the sea at the mercy of lunar cycles—fickle, furious or generous, curling and dilating, forever ignorant of modules, theorems and equations—there appeared these surprising shells, symbolising in number and proportion exactly what the Mother lacked, concrete examples of linear development, of the laws of convolution, of a wonderfully precise conical architecture, of masses in equilibrium, of tangible arabesques which hinted at all the baroquisms to come. Contemplating a snail—a single snail—Esteban reflected on how, for millennium upon millennium, the spiral had been present to the everyday gaze of maritime races, who were still incapable of understanding it, or of even grasping the reality of its presence. (180)

As in the case of the symbolic act of climbing the tree, Esteban is unable to apprehend on a conscious level the significance of the conch shell as it relates to his own participation in history, which he sees only as a negative cycle of endless betrayals. In contrast to the undifferentiated chaos of the maternal womb, the conch shell with its spiral configuration of "linear development" and "laws of convolution" represents a synthesis of continuity and change. For as Ariel Dorfman points out, "history is not a straight line of absolute progress nor is it the ever monotonous circular return of the same; it is the combination of both categories, repetition and progress, movement and immobility, Archetype and chronology: it is the Spiral, repetition with change."[11] The impossibility of evading participation in the historical process dominates the pattern of Esteban's experience in the attempt to get back home to Cuba. He will find that each historical act generates another like the movement of the spiral.[12]

When he returns to Guadeloupe, Esteban discovers that Victor has been discredited in Paris; his privateering operations have provoked the United States to declare war on all French ships in American waters. The Agent of the Directory confesses his own disillusion with the Revolution and offers Esteban a letter of safe-conduct in exchange for the favor of conveying a large sum of money to an old friend in French Guiana. Upon arriving in the French penal colony, Esteban witnesses a world of total moral degradation, which—like the withered Tree of Liberty in front of the Government House—was "a sad, exhausted world, where everything seemed to have been toned down to the somber shades of an etching" (212).

Nevertheless, after carrying out his mission, Esteban has an opportunity to go to Surinam as secret agent for yet another revolutionary government; once there he is to distribute the Decree of Emancipation in order to incite an uprising against the Dutch so that the colony can be annexed by the French. Although Esteban considers this a politically and morally reprehensible act, he volunteers anyway with the intention of not carrying out the plan. Compared to the sordid decadence of Cayenne, Esteban is impressed by Dutch rule in Surinam. But he soon discovers behind the facade of luxury and tolerance a sanitized version of the same inhumanity he had encountered in French Guiana.

Shortly before leaving Surinam, Esteban sees a group of black men under armed guard in a local hospital. To his astonishment, he learns that these men are runaway slaves who have been condemned by the Dutch "Courts of Justice" to have their left legs amputated: "And since the sentence must be cleanly and scientifically carried out, without resort to archaic methods belonging to the age of barbarism and which might cause excessive suffering or endanger the prisoners' lives, the nine slaves had been brought to the best surgeon in Paramaribo, so that he could carry out the court's verdict, saw in hand" (241). Horrified by this example of "enlightened" cruelty, Esteban decides to distribute the Decree of Emancipation among the blacks of Surinam rather than throw them away as he had originally intended. This incident is one of many that will thwart Esteban's efforts to withdraw from the arena of historical action.

After nearly ten years of absence, Esteban returns home to Cuba carrying with him a somber account of the failures of a revolution in which "the Age of the Scaffold had succeeded the Age of the Tree of Liberty" (260). He expresses abhorrence at the number of lives sacrificed in the name of a liberty and a fraternity that had become deceptive political slogans aimed at annexing territory. Bitterly he concludes: "This time the Revolution has failed. Perhaps the next will be the real one. But if they want to find me when it breaks out they'll have to hunt high and low. We must beware of too much fine talk, of Better Worlds created by words. Our Age is succumbing to a surfeit of words. The only Promised Land is that which a man can find within himself" (261).

Esteban's long-awaited homecoming fails, however, to bring him the peaceful reunion he had envisioned. Sofia emphatically rejects his negative assessment of the course of the Revolution. While she expresses sympathy for the pain he has suffered, she attributes his disillusionment to an exaggerated sense of idealism and a partial, limited view of historical developments. Ironically, Esteban finds that "the *ideas* which he had left behind had now caught up with him, in an environment where everything seemed organised to neutralise them" (274). His cousins are consumed by the revolutionary fervor of the very same political tracts he had translated in Guadeloupe and are engaged in disseminating them throughout Cuba. When he later accuses those involved in conspiring against the colonial government of "playing at revolutions," Sofia responds that it is better to play at something than nothing at all (285).

Divided from his cousins by ideological differences and the passage of time, Esteban feels like a stranger in his own home. Sofia and Carlos strike him as too comfortably bourgeois and, in light of his own experience, naively impressed with what he considers outmoded, inappropriate ideas. Carlos is a prosperous, respectable-looking businessman in spite of his revolutionary leanings. The Sofia of his childhood—"the Elder Sister, the Young Mother, the pure feminine entelechy of other times" (254)—is now a grown woman who is to all appearances proud of her well-connected marriage and her role as wealthy "*ama de casa.*" Esteban himself has changed in ways he had not suspected. He finds the family house too orderly, too well cared for; he soon becomes restless and realizes he will never be able to devote the rest of his life to the family business.

Esteban's return coincides with the final days of the Age of Enlightenment; an epidemic that brings the death of Sofia's husband Jorge ushers in the new century.[13] The death of her husband, like the death of her father a little over ten years earlier, brings a new beginning for Sofia. Shortly after the funeral, Esteban discovers her plan to leave Cuba to join Victor Hugues in French Guiana where he has just returned to power. Refusing to heed Esteban's objections, Sofia leaves the family home to enter "an epic world, inhabited by Titans" (290). Despite the archetypal resonances of her departure, there is considerable irony in Carpentier's treatment of Sofia's vision of a heroic mission in Victor's world. Before assuming the role of heroine, she must be tested, as was Esteban, by her own experience of the descent into hell.

Distraught but determined to prevent Sofia from joining Victor, Esteban returns home to find colonial agents searching the house for subversive literature, intent on arresting all of them for conspiracy against the government. In order to protect Sofia, Esteban invents a lengthy, detailed confession that results in his own arrest and deportation. Sacrificing his own freedom, he is drawn back into the historical vortex. Esteban's homecoming cycle ends with the beginning of Sofia'a quest, but the second round is not a mere repetition of the first.

Sofia'a quest completes the triadic structure of the novel. In this regard, Roberto González Echevarría interprets her relationship to Esteban and Victor in the context of the cabalistic symbolism of the Sephiroth: *Kether, Hokmah,* and *Binah.* He identifies Esteban with Kether whose name corresponds to the Greek meaning of *stephanus,* the crown. Kether is the first manifestation of *En-Sof* (God) and represents the counterbalance of the other two forces. Hokmah, the archetype of the father, embodies the will to power, or the "bursting desire to put forth the plan of creation." Binah is the "supernal mother" whose power to differentiate is associated with wisdom, the meaning of Sofia's name. Victor, the surrogate father, and Sofia, the archetypal mother, are therefore identified with Hokmah and Binah respectively; they both serve as catalysts that move the basically passive Esteban into action.[14]

Echevarría concludes that Esteban is the most important member of the triad and that the "whole of the novel" is contained within him. It is important, however, to keep in mind Carpentier's emphasis on history as the interaction or "co-determination" of multiple, often conflicting factors.[15] If anything, it would seem that Sofia represents the countervailing force between Victor's extreme materialism and Esteban's escapist transcendentalism; she understands history as a dialogue between social ideals and social action.

It is also important to distinguish just how Sofia functions as feminine archetype in *El siglo*. She is not the woman Esteban thought she had become on returning home (the complacent *ama de casa*), nor is she the woman he wants her to be (*la mujer elemental*). In spite of her inexperience, Sofia sees herself as an independent woman whose desires go far beyond the limited domestic roles imposed on most women. Like Esteban at the beginning of his quest, she wants to participate in history on a grand scale. She is attracted to Victor because she believes he is a man of "great enterprises." Although she is destined to be disappointed, her vision of revolutionary social change is not dependent on him.

In his description of archetypal Sophia as the vessel of rebirth and transformation, Erich Neumann writes:

> Sophia, who achieves her supreme visible form as a flower, does not vanish in the nirvanalike abstraction of a masculine spirit; like the scent of a blossom, her spirit always remains attached to the earthly foundation of reality. Vessel of transformation, blossom, the unity of Demeter reunited with Kore, Isis, Ceres, the moon goddesses, whose luminous aspect overcomes their own nocturnal darkness, are all expressions of this Sophia, the highest feminine wisdom.

Neumann then distinguishes between the elementary character of the feminine archetype and the transformative character dominant in the Sophia figure: "As spirit mother, she is not, like the Great Mother of the lower phase, interested primarily in the infant, the child, and the immature man, who cling to her in these stages. She is rather a goddess of the Whole, who governs the transformation from the elementary to the spiritual level; who desires whole men knowing life in all its breadth, from the elementary phase to the phase of spiritual transformation."[16]

For the Sofia of *El siglo* spiritual transformation is only possible through human action; the constant refrain in her life is "something must be done." Her wisdom therefore corresponds to Neumann's description of the archetypal Sophia as the goddess who is always willing to intervene;[17] it is the wisdom of the heart rather than the abstract wisdom of the head. In *El siglo,* Sofia functions as both a catalyst (the inspirational anima figure for Esteban) and an active participant in the historical process. Her role in relationship to Esteban and Victor is therefore essential for completing Carpentier's emphasis on social change as a dialectical synthesis of opposing forces.

Sofia's first sea voyage with Victor was interrupted by the outbreak of the Haitian Revolution. Now as she moves toward fulfillment of the new role she has chosen for herself, Sofia commences her second journey with a sense of "penetrating into a timeless present" (301). Rumors of rebellion throughout the Americas seem to confirm her belief that the Great Event she hopes to participate in is already under way:

> To understand this one need only look at a compass-card: from Guadeloupe the squall had blown across to the Guianas, and thence to Venezuela, which was the normal route for getting to the other side of the continent and the baroque palaces of the Kingdom of Peru. It was from there in fact, from the mouths of the Jesuits—Sofia knew the writings of one Vizcardo Guzmán—that the first words had come, demanding independence for these lands which could only be conceived in terms of a revolution. Everything was becoming clear to her: Victor's presence in Cayenne was the beginning of something that would find expression in great troops of horses crossing the plains, in voyages up legendary rivers, in the crossing of high mountain ranges. An age was being born which would accomplish, here in America, what had come to naught in senile Europe. (304–5)

Her mistake, of course, is believing that Victor is the herald of that revolution. When the freemason Caleb Dexter's ship stops in Bridgetown, Barbados, Sofia visits the tomb of a seventeenth-century priest, Ferdinand Palaeologus, a descendant of the last Christian rulers of the Byzantine Empire. Sofia had first heard of this grave site from Victor; therefore, when Dexter refers to the unknown priest as the last legitimate resident of the Basilica of Saint Sophia, she sees the coincidence of names as an omen of a future with Victor, the man of will who would carry out the "Great Task."[18]

With Sofia's arrival in Cayenne, El siglo seems to enter a cycle of repetitions. She finds the same Acadian drunkard shouting the same apocalyptic prophecies that Esteban had encountered when he arrived in the French penal colony. But just as Captain Dexter's ship does not follow the same route, neither does the course of Sofia's journey. Nor will it, however, live up to her own idealistic expectations, which are literally splattered with mud when a herd of wild pigs invades the house where she anxiously awaits Victor. Her torn, mud-splattered clothing contrasts ridiculously with the Mandatory's gleaming military regalia. This humiliating episode is the true omen of Sofia's experience with Victor in French Guiana. For once she goes beyond the deceptive surface of reality, she sees the abasement of all her expectations of this "Great Encounter."

The former Agent of the Directory is now Agent of Bonaparte's Consulate. As in Guadeloupe some six years earlier, Victor has brought order and prosperity to French Guiana. His regime is characterized as "paternalistic and sensible," but there is little evidence of his carrying out any great revolutionary enterprise. He depends on policies handed down in Paris, and it seems that Bonaparte is not so concerned with promoting revolution in the Americas.

At first Sofia is content rediscovering the sexual pleasures of her first encounter with Victor, but she soon begins to experience the same series of disillusionments that had so devastated her cousin Esteban. With the arrival of Roman Catholic monks and nuns in the port of Cayenne, she learns of the Concordat established between Bonaparte and Pope Pius VII restoring Catholicism as the official religion of the state. This reversal of revolutionary policy is then followed by a law reinstituting slavery in the French colonies. Sofia, like Esteban, is horrified by these betrayals of the highest ideals of the French Revolution and the cold matter-of-fact way in which Victor implements them in the name of political necessity:

> All hopes of what she would find there, in this outpost of the new ideas, were turning into intolerable disappointments. She had dreamed of making herself useful amongst men who were fearless, just and firm, and who ignored the gods, because they no longer needed their help, and knew that they were capable of ruling a world which belonged to them; she had thought she would be watching Titans at work, and she had not been afraid of the blood that might be spilled in such a noble cause; but all she was seeing was the gradual restoration of everything which the greatest books of the age had taught must be abolished. Now after the rebuilding of the temples, they were proceeding to the imprisonment of the enchained. And all those who had it in their power to

prevent such things, in this continent where they might still preserve what had been lost on the other side of the Ocean, did nothing at all, because they were too much concerned with their own careers. (321–22)

Sofia witnesses Victor's revolutionary ideals transformed into the mud and stone of extensive building projects. Hundreds of formerly emancipated blacks are forced to begin the recovery of jungle areas for Victor's scheme of "conquering Nature" in French Guiana. Like Christophe in *El reino,* he sees himself as "the Great Architect" but Sofia recognizes the futility of his grandiose plans:

> Sofia deplored Victor's wasting so much energy in a vain attempt to create here, in this virgin forest, which stretched uninterrupted as far as the sources of the Amazon—perhaps as far as the shores of the Pacific—an ambitious simulacrum of a royal park, whose statues and rotundas would be absorbed by the undergrowth the moment they were left untended, and would merely supply support and nourishment for the limitless vegetation engaged in its perpetual task of dislodging stones, splitting stones, splitting walls, breaking open mausoleums, and annihilating the work of human hands. Man wanted to make his puny presence felt in an expanse of green reaching from Ocean to Ocean like an image of eternity. (325)

In disgust Sofia shuts herself up in the house, trying to block out the scene of Victor's building operations. The sense of a timeless present she once felt becomes the dead present of lost illusions. She longs for any event that might shake the colony out of its stagnant reality governed by contracts, harvests, and profits. The event comes in the form of the mass exodus of the reenslaved blacks who, "retracing the course of history," take refuge in the rain forest, and thus fulfill the Swiss planter Sieger's prediction of *una Gran Cimarronada,* the pattern of resistance and flight that had not ceased since the sixteenth century (231). The struggle for freedom among the blacks had begun long before the Pluviose Decree of the Year Two and would continue long after its revocation under the Floreal Law of the Year Ten.

With soldiers from Napoleon's Egyptian campaign, Victor organizes a punitive expedition that recalls Leclerc's Haitian expedition in what would have been the same year (1802). The French soldiers are defeated by forces they cannot see: the hit-and-run tactics of small bands of rebels hidden behind trees in the hostile environment of the jungle and finally by the outbreak of a disease they brought with them from Egypt. Victor is among the sick and wounded to be taken to Cayenne. Delighted by the failure of the expedition, Sofia leaves the stricken Mandatory's hacienda knowing that she will never return; but she refuses to return to Cuba, vowing never to go back to a home she has left in search of a better one.

She wants to return to "the world of the living, where people believe in something" (335). Unlike Esteban, Sofia remains firm in her belief in the possibility of a better world. Her experience with Victor in French Guiana teaches her the ethics of political power— that is, the wisdom to differentiate between acceptable and unacceptable moral behavior in the quest for revolutionary social change. Mistress of her own mind and body, she leaves Victor "having closed, of her own volition, the cycle of a long alienation" (336). Ultimately, Sofia is reunited with her cousin Esteban in Madrid where they sacrifice their lives in the revolt of the Spanish people against the Napoleonic occupation of 1808. Ironically, the Spanish rebellion against the French incites the Latin American wars of independence that Sofia had hoped to participate in with Victor.[19] Through her willing sacrifice, Sofia thus becomes a force of continuity and renewal in the struggle for freedom.

In *El siglo de las luces*, Sofia is the mediator between Victor's absolute materialism and Esteban's abstract idealism. For she recognizes that the process of growth and transformation in history and human consciousness is one of neither linear progression nor circular repetition, but a dialectical synthesis of the temporal and the eternal. In her quest for revolutionary social change, Sofia understands the symbolism of the spiral. She combines the spirit of the mythic and historical imagination in her active pursuit of ideals through social action.

In *Tumatumari*, Wilson Harris brings the conflict between nature and society, intuition and reason, ideology and practice that lie at the center of *El siglo de las luces* into the twentieth century. Harris's novel covers approximately fifty years of Guyanese social history from the post–World War I period to 1967, and like *El siglo* deals with a society in transition from colonialism to independence. Similarly, the history of a middle-class creole family parallels the sociopolitical development of the nation. The merging of family and social history in *Tumatumari,* however, is a reconstructive "act of memory" rather than the lived historical experience portrayed in *El siglo.*[20] The novel highlights the Guyanese response to the failure of colonial and postcolonial social policies. Where *El siglo* opens with the promise of a new beginning ushered in by the Age of Enlightenment and the French Revolution, *Tumatumari* begins with a condition of social, economic, and political collapse.

In *Tumatumari* the triadic structure of the novel in the development of the myth/history relationship revolves around Prudence, whose wisdom is achieved through a difficult process of implosion, Harris's metaphor for creative vision. Since he does not believe in "itinerant novels," the journey toward consciousness is presented as the inward collapse of personality or what he describes as "constantly breaking down things in order to sense a vision *through* things" rather than the conventional notion of plot.[21] Harris's attitude toward plot development in the novel is consistent with his attitude toward the particulars of historical data as fossilized deposits, "static polarizations of cultural identity that confirm our own helplessness in the name of conquests of appearances that enlarge and incapacitate, at the same time, the body politic of a civilization."[22] In novels like *Tumatumari,* he is concerned with exploring potential responses to the basic patterns of history conceived as static "architectonic" space that can only be revised through creative consciousness. The structure of *Tumatumari* is, therefore, one of tentative, shifting images, emphasizing paradoxes and the conversion of opposites.

For Harris social action, participation in the historical process, is the "prison-house of adventure." In the epigraph to another novel he writes: "Since 'adventure' and 'science' have led over many centuries to the denigration of humanity, robot law, unfeeling yoke, there is no ground of alternatives but to recover the 'dangerous' chasm, the 'forbidden' ascent and seek a new dimension of feeling—a new oath of humanity."[23] In *Tumatumari* the reinterpretation of the quest is the recovery of that "dangerous chasm," which is portrayed as the reconstruction of history through the creative "act of memory." Prudence is therefore identified with Mnemosyne, the goddess of memory and mother of the Muses.[24] Compared to Sofia, however, Prudence is a passive anima figure. She is the vessel of consciousness through whom we experience the psyche of the husband and father, but whose own personality has no existence of its own. Hena Maes-Jelinek describes her as the "medium ('vicarious hollow'), in which the past re-enacts itself."[25]

Whereas Carpentier views history as the "battleground of imagination," for Harris history is always the battleground that threatens to crush the spirit of the imagination. In *El siglo* there is a dynamic relationship between inner and outer reality; while in *Tumatumari*, as in Harris's other novels, there is a persistent escape into the psyche away from the material world. Prudence, in a condition of nervous collapse, is isolated in time and space. Harris considers such altered states of consciousness necessary for penetrating the stony formations of history.

The title of the novel is the Amerindian name for "sleeping rocks" and indicates the need to activate the latent energy in the fossilized contents of reality. The emphasis in *Tumatumari* is on the animating force of the creative imagination. Harris's commitment to the psychoanalytic model, however, tends to substitute one static reality for another. The flux of historical interaction is frozen, as it were, in the mind of Prudence. The proposed breakthrough of consciousness is ultimately only tentative. The most problematic aspect of the novel, however, is Harris's tendency toward decontextualization—that is, the construction of novelistic form around an empty center or void, what he refers to as the "concept of the barren."[26]

In *Tumatumari* Harris establishes a paradoxical relationship between barrenness and fertility. The novel opens with Prudence suffering from a nervous breakdown. The delivery of her stillborn child and the death of her husband trigger the psychic collapse that makes her more receptive to the subconscious apprehension of the past. For Prudence, the barren womb is a source of regeneration, the "pregnancy of the void."[27] Thus she sits at the top of the Tumatumari waterfall contemplating the "well of history."

Through memory and her father's unpublished papers, Prudence reconstructs the unknown and misunderstood aspects of her family history, uncovering the inner life behind the mask of creole respectability and gentility. She later recognizes the reassembly of her family history as a dangerous game of "inner space," the penetration of the "spatial womb" in which all desires for sovereignty over self and nature crumble. This disintegration is necessary for the "translation of the Gorgon" (152–53), the symbol of history in *Tumatumari*.

The family history of Prudence Tenby corresponds to Harris's notion of Guyanese and West Indian social history as "New World psyche" buried in polarized conceptions of conquest, but one which nevertheless has a latent capacity for renewal: "Who could tell when IMPLOSION OF GENERATIONS, ROCK WOMB would part, until there emerged, returned—out of a spring that was poisoned—ONE who had spent but a Night beneath the unequal burden of time? Calendar of the muses. Centuries of earth-rape, earth-fear. A day in the flying rock of history speeding with soul's light" (100). Prudence is the alchemical vessel of transformation, the womb of "conception as well as conscience" (49). Through her "adventure into the hinterlands of the ancestors" (152), Harris defines his concept of the relationship between the Guyanese past and future. As she peers into the Well of History, Prudence discerns the "LAMPOSTS OF THE FUTURE WITHIN THE FLYING PRESENT AND PAST" (66) reflected in the lives of her father and husband. Henry Tenby, the historian, is associated with the misconception of the Guyanese past; while Roi Solman, the engineer and man of action, is associated with the need for an accommodation between nature and science in the future.

Prudence was her father's favorite child, born in 1940 but conceived by him as an ideal in 1922 at a time of social crisis when he felt compelled to betray his muse in order to survive. At an early age he recognizes in her the gift of imagination. In order to fulfill her potential, he predicts she will need to marry an engineer, "a Cultural engineer—art and science. That's where the courage for the future lies. . . . Not simply technological descent into matter (vulgar ruin). But a far-reaching assessment of the collision of cultures (nature and society)—the hidden *lapis,* the buried unity of man" (63). However, Prudence's marriage to Roi Solman does not immediately bring about the union of art and science that her father envisioned as the hope of the future.[28] Roi's scientific knowledge is a force of darkness rather than illumination, the "science of night." Conforming to the pattern of the conquest—three centuries of "invasion and penetrative settlement" (134)—he uses his power to exploit the Amerindians of Tumatumari, but his plans for the development of the interior fail. Prudence discovers that he is a "husband of scarce resources" (124) whose faith in modern technology results in an "alienation of cultures," the conflict between nature and society (81). Like Henry Tenby, Roi betrays his muse in the name of self-interest and becomes an "outrider of remorse" (83), Harris's phrase for the legacy of failed social and economic policies.

In Book 1, "The Mask of the Sun," Prudence recalls her marriage to Roi Solman, child of the sun and prince of the waterfall. Their marriage is not only symbolic of the uneasy alliance between art (imagination) and science, but also the difficult relationship between the coastland mentality and that of the interior. Furthermore, the couple's mixed ethnic backgrounds reveal the tragic racial conflicts that divide modern Guyanese society.

They were married in Georgetown after a brief courtship, but even then Prudence suspected that Roi was concealing something from her. Nevertheless, she made the journey upriver from the coast to join him in the house built on stilts in the midst of the rain forest where they lived for little over a year before his death. Their relationship, however, is strained by the presence of Roi's Amerindian mistress Rakka and by his bizarre behavior.

In Georgetown, Prudence saw her future husband's detachment and lack of sentimentality as an admirable "capacity for single-mindedness (nursed by a life of exposure to the elements) . . . an enormous hidden fire" (22), but she finds this same quality threatening in the isolation of the interior. She is disturbed by his sardonic laughter and stony indifference to the plight of others: "Was this lack and deficiency the hidden point of an arrow he turned against others when he laughed, to all appearances, at himself? His wide brutal mouth would crack open, hidden spring coil, charm of immunity. Such incredible innocence, malevolence, objectivity left him unashamed of action (however emotionally and irrationally driven) like a fetish whose powers reflected the penalty as well as prize of immersion" (23). Prudence discovers that Roi's harsh exterior masks the anguish of his own contradictions, which would "rend him in two, invest him with a pitiless destiny" (83). His account of an episode that took place before their marriage gives her some insight into the source of his inner conflict. When shortly after her arrival at Tumatumari she inquires about the possibility of bringing electricity to the area, Roi disdainfully tells her his "technological fable of history" (26).

Five years before Prudence came to Tumatumari, Roi began measuring the discharge of the river above the falls for a hydroelectric project. Because of a scarcity of skilled labor, he had to install an automatic gauge instead of an ordinary pole gauge. He also had to build a well where he could move around in his float, insulated from the wave action of the river. One day while he was digging the well, he slipped and fell, striking his head on the bottom of the concrete framework. The accident resulted in a severe electric shock, from which he claims to have recovered fully, but Prudence is skeptical. Within a day or so of his accident, the river began to rise, flooding the pit. He had to suspend operations until the next dry season, but in the meantime his partners in the new company that was financing the project went bankrupt.

Prudence is both "fascinated and repelled" by the wealth of detail in Roi's tale of the failure of "technological dawn" at Tumatumari, which she compares to the conventional notions of history and realism: "She understood for the first time . . . the 'point' of his 'laughter'—arrow of dimension. A dot on a curve. Statistics of love. Stage discharge curve. Violence and comedy. Call it by any name you like. Convertible rock, tension. Climax of fate, involuntary theatre, eyelid of stone, *lapis* of populations. Awakening of sleepers. Disembodied electric uproar" (26). Thus Roi Solman is associated with the artificial illumination of technology (electricity) and the natural illumination of the sun. Harris describes him as the "Oracle of pitfall and sunstroke" (24). This interpretation of solar consciousness as a blinding, destructive force is consistent with Neumann's characterization of solification as the one-sided, abstract wisdom of the head, in this case scientific knowledge divorced from nature.[29]

Within Harris's archetypal framework, Roi and Prudence therefore represent the active faculties of the masculine solar principle—

reason and will—in contrast to the feminine lunar characteristics, imagination, feeling, and perception. Roi's rocklike persona (solar phallus), however, is "convertible," capable of transformation as are the patterns of history and realism. The title of Book 1, "The Mask of the Sun," suggests this aspect of Roi's consciousness; his is an "opaque sun," which indicates both a state of eclipse and the *Sol niger* of alchemy:

> Alchemists took up this image of the *Sol niger* to symbolize "prime matter", or the unconscious in its base, "unworked" state. In other words, the Sun is then at the nadir, in the depths out of which it must, slowly and painfully, ascend towards its zenith. This inevitable ascent does not relate to its daily journey, although this is used as an image, and hence it is symbolized by the transmutation of prime matter into gold, passing through the white and red stages, like the Sun itself in its orbit.[30]

Prudence, the alchemical vessel of transformation, has a premonition on the same day that she hears Roi's story, which is also the day that she finds out that she is pregnant: "She had a grotesque foreboding (which she tried to stifle) of his coming death by drowning in the falls THROUGH HER (AS IF SHE WOULD SUMMON HIM, PUSH HIM) so that his tale seemed to her to possess a recapitulative guilt of resources past and future—the mystery of the barren rock in the well" (28). Roi's death, like the diurnal passage of the sun, is a symbol of salvation, the rebirth of consciousness.

In life, however, Roi is unable to translate his experience in the well into a new conception of change. Like Donne in *Palace of the Peacock*, he struggles to maintain his position as Sovereign of the Rock by exploiting the Amerindians who work on his land. Furthermore, he betrays their trust by taking advantage of his Amerindian kinship to maintain control over them. He performs the Ceremony of the Rock, a ritual conquest of the waterfalls in which he assumes the role of the hunter of the wild boar of the rapids, reenacting the death of the old king and the birth of a new creation.

Although Roi, like Donne, recognizes the Amerindians as the "conscience of our age," he manipulates their traditions in the name of science, emancipation, and industry but primarily for the preservation of his own self-interest. He argues:

> One must counter spiritual subversion by suspending its own tool. One cannot tolerate breakdown in day-to-day rule. And the Indians under my control will *not* accept it that there's nothing truly consistent remaining to exercise authority over them once the caution (foreboding) exists that such sovereign recognition is degrading. It's a long sad incestuous tale no doubt through which may I remind you we preserve our crops. What little there is. Not only potatoes, but diamonds, gold, meat, fish. The first time I had to contend with defection was five years ago. You remember I fell and nearly broke my neck. Practically surrendered to the ghosts. The unholy Indians had been seen then as now. Luckily events conspired to make a deal with them. I recovered. At a price. By way of the filthy ceremony—the Ceremony of the Rock as the people around the hill call it. We rubbed our noses upon it—metaphorically speaking of course. I was seen as their lighthouse—scapegoat. . . .
>
> . . . After all the object is one of upholding an economic establishment—emancipation, enlightenment—by fair means or foul. (36)

The myths and traditions of the Amerindians are subverted by the "science of night" and treated as so much "garbage to be disposed of upon the frontiers of a technological universe whose stunned premises could now be hidden under a new mantle, a new 'guiltless' emancipation" (48). Roi, however, overestimates his power to control the Amerindians who—like the rebellious maroons in *El siglo de las luces*—continue their pattern of defections.

The next time the Amerindians abandon Tumatumari, Roi leaves for the gold and diamond fields of Mazaruni in search of more laborers. While there he hears news of a Guyana/Venezuela territorial dispute that threatens the very land he defiantly claims as "his own matchless wilderness" (180). During his absence, Prudence delivers their stillborn child. As if compelled by some invisible force, Roi races across country toward Tumatumari and his own death. He is decapitated by the revolving outboard motor of his boat when he collides with a rock in the river rapids near the same place he had his first accident in the concrete pit of the well.

109

Roi's life is emblematic of the misuse of resources, "past and future," repeating the pattern of Henry Tenby's life, which his daughter relives through the "eye of the waterfall" after the death of her husband. The fusion of the memory of the father and the husband represents the legacy of the past in the present and future. Prudence recognizes a resemblance between her father, the historian, and her husband, the engineer. Although they are different in physical appearance and personality, they are dual aspects of the same historical premise:

> Art of control. For the good of the tribe/family. Economics of survival. Pass law. Virtue. Reins upon an underground imagination which they exercised over a life-time of bitterness until from their own lips a heartrending cry arose. . . .
> . . . an ironic unity through incarceration—a century devoted to binding souls in categories of service to an ideal; roping souls, bareback riders, encirclement—all in the name of progress. Ironic indeed because through such bars, reins of the devil, prisonhouse—shone clear at last the political conscience of the race. (46, 86)

Prudence reconstructs her father's life from his postgraduate student days after World War I in 1919 until 1957, the year of his death at the age of sixty. Thus the life of Henry Tenby and his family parallels the development of modern Guyanese social history. Three of his children, Prudence, Hugh, and Pamela—in the reverse order of their actual birth—are described as mental conceptions he adopted in response to the economic, political, and social upheavals of the twenties. They are each associated with analagous historical periods, past and future. The social conflicts of the earlier stage of modernization are repeated with ever-increasing urgency in later decades. Pamela, for example, is associated with the social climate of 1926, 1936, and 1955. Furthermore, each of his three offspring is linked to the different regions and races of Guyana. The Tenby family, like the nation itself, is divided by issues of class, race, and ideology. Prudence, Hugh, and Pamela, therefore, express three modes of response to Guyanese reality.

Henry Tenby was the son of a rice farmer who sacrificed everything he owned so that his son could earn a degree in history. The young Tenby left Guyana for North America where he studied for three years and then went to Europe in 1919 for postgraduate work. On his way to London, he stopped in Marseilles where he met and fell in love with Isabella, symbol of the cultural legacy of Europe and the glittering promise of the new century:

> It had seemed to him in purity and outline—one eye cast backward toward the mud of war—one eye cast down, demure, lashes of gold—the muse of the century. He fell head over heels in love with IT, with her. With the scent of the chase, tatters of reality.
>
> The banner floated above him and then fell like her dress into his arms. He laid it aside—kissed her upon her breasts. The gold of her flesh. Sheer tumultuous fantasy. . . . The desire to buy her like a whore had crossed his mind even as the idealism of love flared, to buy her like baggage in the train of war. (88–89)

Tenby squanders his father's hard-earned money on this "banner of illusion" and takes her with him to London where one evening she suddenly vanishes in the darkness. Stunned by her disappearance, he feels both love and hatred for her:

> She was beautiful, she was ugly. She was slender as a dancer, shackled like a slave, clothed in his rags, prisoner of his womb, self-made Harbour, nature's Rock, man-made Dungeon, Tower of Constraint, Famine of Resources. Something so sovereign and wild, pure and impure, inexpressibly rational, irrational it drove him to extremes—extremity of loathing and desire—extremity of bitter freedom, bitter incarceration of the senses. . . . Half-priestess, half-whore. . . . Every penny he had dug from his pocket to give to her had returned to strike him a ringing blow in the end—decapitation—blessing and curse. (91–92)

Tenby's disappointing affair with Isabella is typical of the experience of many young West Indian students who left the colonies to be educated in Europe. His susceptibility to the charms of this priestess/whore influences his future response to the reality back home. When he returns to Guyana in 1921, he finds his homeland in a state of economic decline: "Delapidated door. Georgetown. It seemed to hang upon the hinges like a raw fist. . . . The blow of recession fell—as if a gateway stood, masked by the centuries upon which one collided. Devaluation of resources (flesh and blood) in the name of principle. Devaluation of principle (flesh and blood) in the name of resources. Barren circuit of gold which began to flicker and run, trade of the imagination" (93).

On his return Tenby begins to wear the mask of virtue and propriety behind which he hides his secret desires. By day he assumes the air of a refined creole gentleman; by night he frequents the brothels of Lombard Street where he buys the favors of women like Rakka, "whore of the past and future" (95). She is Isabella's Amerindian counterpart but also the "guardian of consciousness" who will reappear years later as his son-in-law's mistress. Thus in 1922, in the Brothel of Masks, Tenby adopts the principle that will govern the rest of his life:

> Vow of control. He would scheme and plot for science, security, self-containment. Anything to avoid explaining the callous of history, the stranglehold he detected upon Rakka's flesh and blood. Could she (Prudence) after all—major conception of his life—plumb this cross of inheritance, the trampled banner of freedom, humiliation in the name of order, control: in the name of ticket of ages, price-tag of the year, burning statistic, devaluation, ROCK WOMB, population implosion? . . . Mask of the Waterfall. Conception of Prudence. Rock of History. Collision with a whore. (96)

Henry Tenby's conception of Prudence is thus the fruit of "anguish and self-preservation" (96). Two years later in 1924, he conceives her brother Hugh Skelton. Actually born in 1938, Hugh is the Tenby family's "skeleton in the cupboard," a throwback to their African origins. Scorned because of his blackness, he is given the worst household chores and sent to his room when visitors come. The father's protests are ignored by the rest of the family who understand only too well his vow of self-control and patience.

The year Tenby "conceived" his son Hugh was one of fear and sorrow, marked by widespread disease, economic depression, labor unrest, and police repression:

> Unidentified Flying Objects had appeared in the sky of Conception 1924. Horsemen of the Well—the ghosts of historian and engineer

flying backwards from the future. Hearse of the Waterfall flying for-wards from the past. COLLISION IMMINENT. 1924—Conception of the Negro. Black Health. 1924—Cathedral of Sickness. White Span-ish: Influenza. 1924—Factory of Despair. Strike. Lock-out. Riots. Green Death. Morning Sickness—Colony of the Rainbow. Seed-Time and Harvest. (97)

In the days following the riots of 1924, Henry Tenby returns to the Brothel of Masks. This time his prostitute is an underweight, under-nourished "waif of the docks and streets." The glittery promise of Isabella is now a "goddess of urine and starlight" (101). With her he seals a treaty of evasion that will have disastrous consequences for both his family and nation:

He saw now he had succumbed to FEAR, fear of the deepest confronta-tion with the shackles of humanity, fear of the total transplantation of himself, voyage of himself, expenditure of all he possessed. He was Eurasian (Amerindian on the wrong side of the blanket) and though he never directly confessed it, afraid of his African cargo. African momen-tum, African legacy. . . .

. . . In averting his eyes therefore from the African past—in con-spiring with conventions and allies—Henry Tenby had, without per-ceiving it, confessed to something upon which he, too, collided (Meta-physical Rock) and which drew him through a Conception of War, Treaty of Industry to an Engine of Remorse in advance of its time. (102–3)

Trapped by fear and the need for money, Tenby is unable to give an honest response to the demands of his age. For him the dilemma is: "How to convert rumour into money and pretend at the same time history isn't an unfulfilled bargain between a mob and a bank" (106). Since he cannot write the truth, he decides to compromise his muse; what he needs is "a mask of refinement, a skeleton in the cupboard beautifully preserved" (106). The choice is a catastrophic one, result-ing in the "thirty-three years seizure of his tongue—1924–1957" by the waif of the streets (107).

Tenby makes his final compromise in 1926 when he conceives Pamela, the beautiful daughter of "perfection" and "virtue," during a period of severe drought and global depression:

The time was ripe for such a treaty with Abstraction—an age when difficulty and squalor were too great to face or bear. An age when taxes began to grow and mankind (having just emerged from his chain of scarcity of numbers) began to expand in formation of ghetto towards a horizon where he must diminish the populations of his fear and discover a true order and freedom or else crush himself again: the truth was he (mankind) had adventured little save to retreat into straitjacket, coastland in the name of absentee landlord, China dog for sale, Blackamoor for sale, Wall Street, Bond Street, empty cross for sale. (130)

The conception of Pamela is the opposite extreme of the cruelty and violence Tenby feared: "a formal perfection, a formal petition which set up a new problem, a new area of self-deception" (142). As a result, he retreats further into silence and abstraction, "in sealing his lips like an artifice of popular demand, obedience, non-involved camera, RADIO SKELETON. Committed to formal documentary, skinflint essays, historical attributions which were bland and persuasive, vested interest. Committed, yes, in this fashion: but in spite of all—drinking in a secret wavelength from the future—Theatre of Nervous Breakdown—hum of the grotesque" (129).

Tenby adopts a passive, "non-party, non-vocal" position toward social and political participation. He does not resist the autocratic measures of the British Crown Colony government in 1926, nor will he oppose the suspension of the Liberal Constitution in 1953. The tragic consequences of his retreat into silence is the breakup of the family and the nation, culminating in the social and political collapse of the 1960s.[31]

In the 1920s the future of Henry Tenby's children is "impaled on the ramparts of inner space" (134). His daughter Pamela, born in 1936, rejects his patient economic sacrifice and her homeland. At the age of eighteen she creates a family scandal by getting pregnant and marrying a rich American disc jockey. In the United States she passes for white; when she gives birth to a black child, she gives him up for adoption in order to continue living out an illusion. In Pamela, Tenby's treaty of silence rebounds into "a camouflage of origins" and a "ghetto of self-interest" (131). The beautiful, vain Pamela—like her mother Diana—represents the classical (conventional) conception of art and life ruled by control and logic. In the context of Guyanese social development, she represents the colonial mask of evasion and self-hatred, "an interior negative sphere of action and reaction" (145).

Tenby's son Hugh, the black "skeleton in the cupboard," is born in 1938 and shot down in the streets of Georgetown in 1962. The year of his death, like the year of his imaginary conception in 1924, is one of economic crisis and riots. His life is the tragic result of his father's "fatal miscalculation" in the twenties, the attempt to shove reality underground and postpone confrontations:

> Sum and sun of all his hopes—*Hugh Skelton lying upon his bier . . . Budget Riots* 1962. The shock of confrontation, of standing upon a frontier of frozen resources—frozen profits—broke him into two to confirm his state or constitution $1 + 1 = 0$. As if the bullet which had been fired, had, in fact, been made of diamond and gold (astronomical sums had been inscribed upon it—ammunition works, ammunition dumps—export/import—logarithms of tragic comedy $2 \times$ infinity, serials of comic perspicacity pee squared infinity) and still it equalled nought. As if the score had been masked long ago by his own barren skull, had been fused long before Hugh was born in his own barren breath and written with an economical nib of lust upon the cruel waif of the streets—*Message for Hugh Skelton. This bullet fired by your father's rich kith and kin—all races of endeavour—white + brown + black.* (120)

Hugh is the "rebellious fire" that erupted during the transition to independence in the 1960s as a result of the failure to achieve the cultural and political integration of the various racial and ethnic groups of Guyana.[32] The legacy of racial conflict, cultural fragmentation, and self-interest is the political violence of the future.

Earlier in the novel, Prudence recalls an episode that took place in 1952, ten years before her brother's death. While she slept on the backseat of the family car, her father was driving to Port Mourant on the Courantyne coast when he almost ran over an East Indian woman who was on her way back from work in the rice fields. Upon arriving at Port Mourant, they hear a speech addressed to the People's Progressive Party (PPP) by Comrade Block. The political spokesman, described as "anyone and no-one," uses Tenby's near collision with the East Indian woman as a metaphor of the "hit-and-run" tactics of Guyanese social policies. He sums up the failure of those policies as follows:

> "Let us review our economic position," Comrade Block said. "Not enough labour forty years ago. The lack of an immigration policy led to that. The lack of the reverence for life as Schweitzer would say. Quick profits and be damned. Then came the depression. Further bottle-neck. The interior? Who could dream of the development of the interior? Where was the labour to come from? And the risk anyway for the coastland was too great. Keep the pool steady. Labour must remain at our command. Now the tide appears to have turned. There's more hands than we need. Forgive me if I sound crude. So we must reject. Put a smooth face on it. No longer short supply, short in demand. Put a smooth face on it. Keep the mask in place. Conceal the sickness, corruption. Sell anything once it improves the complexion. Pick and choose. *Reject.* Keep the mask in place. Smooth operation. Slam the bloody brake." (75)

Comrade Block's name suggests the "Rock of History" and the reference to his speech as the "half-truths, half-lies in Everyman's throat" (76) underscores Harris's lack of faith in social action based on what he considers monolithic interpretations of history. The author's use of duality and ambiguity is further illustrated by the role of Prudence, born in 1940 but conceived mentally by her father in 1922. Henry Tenby's conception of Prudence has both negative and positive dimensions. In its original manifestation, his "vow of control" represents the excessive caution that led to a betrayal of consciousness in the 1920s out of fear and self-interest. This conception, however, contains the seeds of wisdom or vision, which he passes on to his daughter at the time of his death. As he dies, one hand strikes Prudence on the forehead, symbolically illuminating his life and the "true state of the *family* to which she belonged" (58).

Prudence's name, like that of Sofia in *El siglo de las luces*, functions as a numen of consciousness. As a child she inscribes her name on the "chair of history" in her father's study as she will later on the rock face of her husband's abandoned well, where she experiences a sense of oneness with nature:

Thus it was that a skeleton film of internal and external organization glowed and occupied her own passive body as she occupied in turn the chair of the well—genesis of function—height as well as depth. An enormous excitement gripped her—authenticity—in which her being, the being of the well, the being of the sky seemed to enfold itself and yet release itself like the unravelling, ravelling petals of a flower. *Disintegrative as well as integrative, ending as well as beginning:* hard engineering words (metaphysical as well as concrete) to emerge in concert with the rose of the jungle, upon a ruin of time which seemed in that instant to belong, less to a technological age—bankrupt uniformity—than to a genuine weakness of space, art and science (overlapping spheres whose interpenetration however flickeringly possessed a light of correspondence between flesh and stone, spirit and rubble) "vision of creation—frailty and dust—which came in itself before the "invention" of the sun. (29–30)

This image of the flowering of consciousness signals her role as womb of conception. Through Prudence, Henry Tenby achieves the "translation of the Gorgon of History." This process of transformation takes place in her reenactment of his life through memory:

It was as if a lowering of horizons had occurred within which a new technological age of Compassion was being born in the heart of the dead past, present and future. A lowering of horizons through which and within which could occur an extrapolation of living resources. . . . Translation of "weakness" (give-and-take) into expanding resources (womb of space). . . . community of resources drawing the heights into the depths, the depths into the heights: resources compressed and translated (transmuted) because of their capacity for diminution as well as elongation, into an infinitesimal opening, crack, eye upon a prison wall, eye within the fastness of pride, ironic grain of sand, rumble of reality, egg-shell. So infinite these resources they possessed an undying chain of splendour to be seized upon afresh whatever the duration of tension, Gorgon or Stone. *Agonising conversion of tongues pointing to a resumption of the conversation with the Muse.* (113–14)

The final image in *Tumatumari* is that of Prudence plunging into the "heart of the whirlpool," the locus of community where the fossilized material of history is transformed:

117

As Prudence began to drown in her multiple Rock of associations the forces of nature long impaled on the ramparts of inner space began to disband their army of conscripts and dissolve into incredible strokes. Incredibly tragical virtues, deflowering of masks—incredibly distant goals, incredibly barren hopes of mortal and immortal riches. . . .

. . . And yet with each fluid bubble the Gorgon's head smiled, wreathed by the elements. (155)

The transformation of history in *Tumatumari* is like the novel itself, a "Game of Conception," the alliance of nature and society through the art of the imagination. Prudence's reconstruction of the past in *Tumatumari* is described as a "spiral of re-discovery and creativity" (62). Her descent into the whirlpool is therefore a descent into consciousness that makes possible the transformation of the "perspective of the Gorgon" (129) identified with colonialism, economic underdevelopment, racial conflict, and the political betrayals of the post-Independence period.

As in *El siglo de las luces*, history in *Tumatumari* is associated with masculine consciousness and images of stone, the petrified record of human endeavor, or what Henry Tenby refers to as the "Sarcophagus of Industry" (64). In both novels, history is a "convertible rock," susceptible to change through the mythic imagination.[33] For Harris, however, this metamorphosis is only possible in the creative realm of art. In *Tumatumari*, he presents an essentially dystopic vision of history (the negative pole of the whirlpool or spiral). In *El siglo de las luces*, on the other hand, the creative force of the imagination includes social ideals as the positive motivation for change in human thought and action even though historical conflict is never completely eradicated.

The descent into the temporal vortex of historical memory is also the subject of Edouard Glissant's *La case de commandeur* (The overseer's hut, 1981). This novel, like *Tumatumari*, is about a Caribbean woman on the edge of the abyss. Marie Celat (Mycéa) has fallen into madness, the final break between self and intolerable otherness in a society that has reached a social and political impasse, *la société bloquée* of modern Martinique in the late 1970s. This is the period of the French doctrine of economic assimilation, which results in the dismantling of the sugar-based economy of the plantation era and transforms the island into a nonproductive tertiary economy totally dependent on France. The politics of 1946 and the modernization schemes of the postwar period only lead to progressive *underdevelopment* of the island. Mycéa's madness is her "rage of refusal" against a long line of losses, betrayals, and aborted acts of rebellion that not only block the path toward an independent Martinique but also undermine personal and family relationships.

Mycéa's madness suggests the "verbal delirium" of the text, which is a descending spiral of repetitions and parallel story fragments presented in a profusion of narrative and stylistic forms. Two newspaper excerpts from the West Indian daily, *Quotidien des Antilles*, dated 4 and 13 September 1978, serve as a narrative frame that indicates the connection between Glissant's social and fictional discourse. The two excerpts include eyewitness accounts of a local woman's deranged behavior and the summary of an optimistic government report on mental health care on the island. The "official" story stands in ironic contrast to the rest of the text, which is a collection of stories within stories about the Celat family and the history of the Martinican peasantry. These stories move backward in time from 1928 (birth of Mycéa) to the trauma of the original uprooting and violent insertion into a New World, the *"Mitan du temps"* (middle of time), which is also the center of the text. The novel then takes up the immediate events leading to Mycéa's breakdown and her recovery.

Just as Prudence does in *Tumatumari*, Mycéa looks into the stony chasm, *la roche de l'opacité*. But her search is a conscious and, as we shall see later, even guided attempt to recover the "ghosts of the past." Where Prudence's memory is involuntary recall provoked by dreams, hallucinatory visions, and other manifestations of the unconscious, Glissant's psychotherapeutic model in *La case* draws directly on the relationship between memory and speech (*la parole*, the spoken word) as a means of reconstructing history and story. As Papa Longoué says in one of the epigraphs to the novel, *"la parole a son histoire qu'il faut fouiller longtemps comme un plant d'igname loin au fond de la terre* [the spoken word has its history which must be dug up a

119

long time like a yam planted deep in the ground]."[34] The search for
the meaning of the word *Odono* is what connects the fragmented
components of Glissant's text.

The novel continues where *Quatrième* and *La Lézarde* leave off, the
period after World War II and the heady, optimistic days of the 1945
elections. Mycéa stands out among her peers because of her remote-
ness and her skepticism about political theorizing. She is a fierce,
outspoken young woman who, like Sofia in *El siglo*, prefers action to
words. Although she is outraged by the seemingly endless series of
political betrayals, unlike most of her friends Mycéa refuses to leave
the island for France.

During this period of disillusionment, Papa Longoué's match, *le
trait d'union*, between Mycéa and Mathieu also fails. Their relationship had always been based on conflicting ways of expressing a shared
passion—the recovery of a buried past:

> Mathieu produisait en idées ou en mots ce que Mycéa gardait au plus
> intouchable d'elle-même et défoulait par bouffées en grands balans de
> vie exagérée. La remontée dans *cela* qui s'était perdu: comment une
> population avait été forgée . . . [des Nègres] traités nus sans une arme
> sans un outil à emporter; comment, venue de tant d'endroits divers et
> tombée là (ici) par les obligations du marchandage et du profit, elle
> s'était accroupie sur elle-même et avait perduré; comment elle avait, à
> partir de tant de mots arrachés ou imposés, sécrété un langage; com-
> ment elle s'usait . . . à oublier. (*La case* 188)

> (Mathieu produced in ideas or in words what Mycéa kept in the most
> untouchable part of herself and released with great swirling gusts of
> exaggerated life. Bringing to the surface *what* had been lost: how a
> people had been forged . . . traded naked without one weapon without
> one tool; how, coming from so many different places and landing there
> (here) out of the demands of bargaining and profit, they had crouched
> over into themselves and had endured; how they had, starting from so
> many snatched and imposed words, created a language; how they wore
> themselves out . . . forgetting.)

The closer the couple comes to penetrating this oblivion, the more
distant they become from one another. Glissant presents the problem
between Mycéa and Mathieu as a conflict between the abstract intellectual control of historical knowledge and the need for a different

kind of engagement with the past. Mycéa does not try to "rule over things with words," and she resents Mathieu for "translating" into words what she already understood, since words are "so foreign to what one accumulates inside oneself like rocks" (*La case* 189, 190).

Unable to bridge the gap, *le trou*, between words and experience, they separate. Mathieu leaves for France, and Mycéa sinks into what she calls an "ordinary, banal" existence, marked by an endless series of sexual liaisons. She has two sons by a man she hardly knows and becomes increasingly withdrawn from her friends and family. She is described as both "*claire et morte*," mentally lucid and emotionally dead. Although Mycéa is said to have looked further into the void, *le trou*, than any of the others of her generation, she is still unable to make sense out of what she recognizes as the passing of the culture of the plantation era—"the uprooted trees, the altered voices, the extinct rhythms" (*La case* 224).

In this state of nearly total alienation, Mycéa takes to wandering by the sea. Drawn to those places where she could make out Dominique to the north or Saint Lucia to the south, she calls out to all of the islands, inviting them to a conference, a joint meeting. These tirades by the sea are another indication of a need to connect with an absence or a lack (*manque*)—the broken link between the islands of the Caribbean archipelago and the awareness of a shared history. The period of Mycéa's growing sense of estrangement, from 1958 to 1978, is one of intense political change and accelerated decolonization in Africa and other areas of the Caribbean; but this "news from elsewhere" finds no echo in Martinique, which appears bogged down in an unproductive economy, and unproductive lives (*La case* 212).

Mycéa's final breakdown is brought on by the death of her two sons, Patrice (named for African independence leader Patrice Lumumba) and Odono (a name of unknown origin passed down from generation to generation of the Celat family). Mycéa's invocation of the word *Odono* as she roams the streets and highways suggests that the roots of her psychic disturbance are even deeper than the loss of her sons:

Elle cherchait quelqu'un ou quelque chose, elle ne savait encore. . . .
Pourquoi faut-il chercher si loin? Si loin dans les espaces dans les amas

de jours et de nuits. Parmi nous parmi nous. Soudain la lumière se brisa, le cri prit forme, elle épela: Odono. Elle cria: Odono, où est Odono? (*La case* 217)

(She was searching for someone or something, she did not know yet. . . . Why must she search so far? So far into the spaces into the mass of days and nights. Among us among us. Suddenly the light broke, the scream took shape, she spelled: Odono. She shouted: Odono, where is Odono?)

The word *Odono* is the fragment of a forgotten past, part of the Celat family history and by extension the collective history of the island. In order to regain her sanity, Mycéa must uncover the repressed knowledge of this past, *le refoulé historique,* that manifests itself as dislocated, fragmented psyche.[35]

When she is committed to a mental institution, located on the border between the forest and the savannah, Mycéa associates the road to the hospital with *"la Trace du Temps d'Avant,"* the road or Path of Former Time. It is in the mental hospital that she meets the person who is the "specialist" in curing what ails her—Chérubin, the crazy man who haunts the abandoned sugar factory. Mycéa escapes from the hospital into the forest with Chérubin leading the way, all the while carrying on his incoherent, delirious discourse about the "voice" and the "family way." He takes Mycéa to an old, deserted overseer's hut, *la case du commandeur,* where he tells her that the only way to overcome her grief, to heal her mind, is *"monter le temps comme un vaillant cavalier si tu ne veux pas que le temps te monte comme un zébu* [to mount time like a valiant rider if you don't want time to mount you like a zebu]" (*La case* 233).

The *case du commandeur* is the site of recovery, the place where Mycéa goes back over the path of time, *la trace du temps d'avant,* toward all she "did not know" about her forebears, as far back as the ancestor Eudoxie in the 1700s. Together, Mycéa and Chérubin "jump over the rocks of time," reliving the story, or rather the stories of the Celat family, which are also the history of the collective "we" (*le nous*):

Ils remontent la Trace du Temps d'Avant. C'est pour nous éclairer, disait Chérubin. J'étais dans le conte, je rêvais que je rêvais. Je com-

prends ça, disait Chérubin. Non non, il n'y a pas de fin, ne dites pas
que vous comprenez, dites que vous avez crié tout au long de la Trace.
J'ai crié, disait Chérubin. Nous avons entendu ce Bruit de l'Ailleurs,
feuilleté toi et moi l'Inventaire le Reliquaire. Nous avons couru ce
Chemin des Engagés, dévalé le Registre des Tourments ho il reste à
épeler le Traité du Déparler. Qu'est-ce que le Traité, demandait Chérubin. C'est le mot mis dans la terre que vous retournez. (*La case* 235)

(They go back over the Path of Former Time. To enlighten ourselves,
Chérubin said. I was in the tale, I was dreaming that I was dreaming. I
understand that, Chérubin said. No no, there's no end, don't say you
understand, say that you have screamed all along the Track. I have
screamed, Chérubin said. We have heard this News from Elsewhere,
you and I have gone through the Inventory the Reliquary. We have run
over this Road of Indenture, run down the Register of Torments oh we
still have to spell out the Treatise of Un-Speaking. What is the Treatise, Chérubin asked. It's the word in the ground that you turn over.)

The recapitulation of the past that takes place in the overseer's hut is
the text we read and the story we must reconstruct in much the same
way that Mycéa does as she plunges into the vertigo of memory.

Thus the text winds back on itself (*s'enroule*), hooking up the voices
of Chérubin and Mycéa with the voice of collective memory in the
opening passages of the novel. The voice of the "we" narrator serves
as commentator, interrogator, and guide through the spiral labyrinth
of stories and story fragments. Through this experiment with the
first-person *plural* narrator, Glissant works against a Western tradition (both in myth and the modern novel) that tends to isolate the
individual from the community. The source of Mycéa's alienation is
not conflict with her community but the lack of community. The
"we" narrator stands as a constant reminder of this absence. *La case
du commandeur* is Glissant's attempt to write *le roman de l'implication*,
the novel of the "we" implied or implicated in the "I."[36] The voice of
the "we" narrator opens and closes the novel and participates as a
reflexive, speculative presence in each of the stories about scattered,
disconnected selves who share the same "ignorance and its haunting
opposite (desire)" (*La case* 30).

In her search for the meaning of Odono, Mycéa recalls the life of
her father Pythagore, the "midday sorcerer" who walks down the

middle of the road shouting the same strange word, not far from where his daughter some forty or fifty years later would struggle to "herd back together the cracked troop of her remembrances" (*La case* 20). Thus the past is projected into the future, merging the events of 1928 (the year of Mycéa's birth) with those of 1978.

Pythagore proclaims the birth of his daughter by blowing on the conch shell (*lambi*), a ritual usually associated with death.[37] Mycéa's birth is mourned by her father because she is not the son he wants, and indeed feels he is entitled to have as his firstborn. Nor as it turns out does she behave like a "real daughter," obediently submissive to her father's authority; her presence even as a very young child is a continual torment to Pythagore. Mycéa is an uncanny, bold child who inherits her mother Cinna Chimène's pride and independence. Daughter and mother are like those other indomitable women in *Quatrième*, Louise and Stéfanise, who have special knowledge and powers that exceed those of their men.[38] Implicit in Pythagore's relationship to Mycéa and Cinna Chimène is a critique of male notions of mastery and control.

Mycéa's presence intensifies the obsessive fears and desires that her father associates with the word *Odono*. He would put his "obscure" questions to anyone he came across and spent his evenings in the local bar where he would inquire if anyone could tell him about Guinea or Congo. In response to his always unanswered question, he would invent his own vision of this place no one knew anything about. Since he has no other points of reference, Pythagore's imaginary Africa very much resembles the only land he knows (*le pays ici*, this land here)—but, of course, the former homeland is a place of abundance and there is a king, *le Roi des Nègres*. Filling in the gaps of what he does not know with desire, Pythagore creates his own myth of Africa.

This illiterate peasant searches for some trace of *le pays d'avant*, the former country, in his daughter's schoolbooks, projecting his dream of Africa onto maps of Brittany and Alsace. Mycéa stubbornly refuses to assist her father in his search:

Il ne savait pas (et il ne savait pas que Mycéa le savait déjà . . .) que les livres n'ont cessé de mentir pour le meilleur profit de ceux qui les produisirent; que ce pays qu'il désirait connaître il lui eût fallu le retrouver en lui-même, par-delà toute description et tout détail. (*La case* 34)

(He did not know [and he didn't know that Mycéa knew already . . .] that books have never ceased to lie for the greater profit of those who produce them; that this country he wished to know he had to find in himself, beyond all description and all detail.)

Pythagore is forced to give up his search for Africa in the schoolbooks; but when he overhears talk of a real African king who had been deported to Martinique around the turn of the century, he decides to track down his king.[39] This new search takes him to the government information bureau where he is rebuffed by petty officials totally indifferent to his story about the African king and contemptuous of a field worker who has pretensions of doing research. His access to books and official records blocked, Pythagore loses the possibility of ever distinguishing between the landscape of the former country and the landscape of Martinique. All that remains of his torment is the obstinate stammering of the word *Odono*.

Pythagore's pursuit of Africa may be read as parody of the myth-making process itself, with its fabulous connections between the real and the imaginary based on improbable parallels and analogies. It may also be interpreted as a critique of some representations of Africa in Caribbean fiction and poetry in the 1920s and 1930s. But despite the humorous details in Glissant's account of this peasant's search to clarify the unknown, there is an undeniable affirmation of his need to know, the desire to recover what has been erased from memory and historical record.

The longed-for "description and detail" that would make Africa *present* in the books is not enough to fill the void expressed in Pythagore's desire to know. This void—the impossible memory of "a catastrophe . . . which the word Odono summed up" (*La case* 44), destabilizes the family, coming between man and woman, parent and child. Pythagore and Cinna Chimène separate, just as Mycéa and Mathieu will years later, because they are unable to understand that they suffer from an "identical sickness," the same absence (*manque*).

The Pythagore section of *"Trace du temps d'avant"* ends with a

125

dramatic account of the moment when ten-year-old Mycéa decides to teach her father how to read. The relationship between literacy and orality in the struggle to fill the void of "primordial trauma," the experience of catastrophe and dispossession in Caribbean history, is one of the basic problems alluded to throughout the novel. The Celat family's obssession with deciphering the meaning of the word *Odono* is thus another occasion for exploring how to tell a history or story impossible to relate in the neatly arranged chronology and plot sequence of traditional narrative.

In *La case* Glissant repeatedly calls attention to his own textual procedures; and part of the difficulty of this complexly structured novel, besides his experiments with the multiple perspectives of the first-person plural narrator, is his attempt to combine the methods of orality and writing in the storytelling process. Orality is *inscribed* in the language as well as the structure of Glissant's text—in his use of long, unpunctuated sentences, frequent repetition and parenthetical digression, rhetorical questions and statements, and collage of narrative episodes. While at the same time, the "we" narrator's commentaries and speculative reflections and the general use of the self-referential language of writing emphasize the literary nature of the text.[40]

The Celat family legends about the grandfather killed by the mule named Mackandal, the mysterious appearance of the foundling Cinna Chimène in the forest, the tale of the Great Fish Chamber, the flying bed and the "miracle mirror" of the great hurricane at the turn of the century are all related with the humor and exaggeration of the folktale, often recalling those techniques associated with the marvelous realism of Carpentier in *El reino* and Gabriel García Márquez in *Cien años de soledad*. There are intimations of the fantastic and supernatural in Glissant's tales of ordinary peasants and slaves whose world is constrained by poverty, uncertainty, and violence. Objective history, though barely alluded to in the text, is manifested in the daily struggles of a people buried in anonymity. These "plantation stories" are verbal feats that defy the destructive force of history and oblivion aimed at putting an end to voices of resistance, like the planter who stuffs a firebrand in the mouth of the first *Négateur* identified with the Odono legend.

126

One of the key stories in *La case* about strategies of resistance and the recovery of the past with words is "Reliquaire des Amoureux" (Lovers' reliquary), the story of Anatolie Celat, the first of Mycéa's ancestors to "earn" a family name. Anatolie, a wanderer and prodigious lover from the age of twelve, is a "sower of stories" and children (he has some thirty-six sons and daughters). This legendary lover and raconteur seduces every woman he meets by telling each of them just part of a story he heard from his grandmother Eudoxie. His slave master, also a philanderer, gets the bits and pieces of Anatolie's "chopped up tale" from the same women; and then relates what he hears to his wife who becomes obsessed with piecing the story together into some kind of coherent whole. But Anatolie's "broken stories" subvert the slave mistress's notion of logic and control, "chasing History right off her desk" (*La case* 155).

The only woman able to recompose Anatolie's story is Liberté Longoué, daughter of the quimboiseur Melchior. She takes the story back toward its beginning but finds that the beginning is lost in obscurity—"*dans un trou sans fond,*" in a bottomless pit. The beginning of Anatolie's story can never really be established because as Papa Longoué says in *Quatrième,* there is always a time before (33). Liberté's reading of the pieced-together story reveals a complex, ambiguous tale, which parallels the one about her own ancestor, the first maroon of the Longoué line.

Anatolie's *histoire éclatée* mirrors the fragmented, de-centered discourse of Glissant's novel as a whole, in which as the "we" narrator says,

> déferla sur nous la foule des mémoires et des oublis tressés, sous quoi nous peinons à recomposer nous ne savons quelle histoire débitée en morceaux. Nos histoires sautent dans le temps, nos paysages différents s'enchevêtrent, nos mots se mêlent et se battent, nos têtes sont vides ou trop pleines. (*La case* 126)

> (the horde of memories and wreathed oblivion unfurled upon us, beneath which we struggle to recompose we don't know what story cut up in pieces. Our stories jump in time, our different landscapes get mixed up, our words get jumbled and fight against each other, our heads are empty or too full.)

During her seance with Chérubin in the overseer's hut, Mycéa penetrates the stony pit of memory until she reaches the "*Mitan du temps*" (Middle of time), the space in the past where all narration and chronology break down. Here she experiences the inward collapse of memory or process of implosion, to use Harris's term, that will lead to her cure. This is also the middle of Glissant's text and the most disjunctive part of the novel, composed of several story segments about the "forgotten, unspeakable truths" in a history of violation and repeated acts of resistance that are often futile but unending.

These tales of rupture and resistance in *Mitan du temps* go back to the remote past, probably at the beginning of the slave trade in the earliest days of the settlement of the island, when the first *Négateur* of the Celat family escapes into the woods only to be betrayed and burned alive. Although the rebel gives himself the name "AA" after the first sound of the white man's language, he is one of two Africans named Odono. Before dying, the rebel tells his story of a friendship destroyed by jealousy and betrayal. One brother sells the other into captivity but—like the Longoué and Béluse ancestors in *Quatrième*— they both end up on the slave ship. No one ever knows whether the executed *Négateur* was the betrayer or the betrayed, nor who are the descendants of which brother. This story of doubles represents the collective history of the people who came on the slave ships, which is then transformed over time into the tale of the Great Fish Chamber, the folk version of betrayal, captivity, and the Middle Passage. The legend of Odono, of which only the name remains, is yet another version of this collective (hi)story.

Glissant's text suggests that the recovery—the psychic retrieval of the history of the Odono legend and Mycéa's cure—can only take place in the *Mitan du temps,* the vertiginous descent into the shattered space of memory. And to use the other image in the text, Mycéa and Chérubin are the "stonebreakers" of time who pound the rock of history (the memory blocks) to dust in order to achieve a transformation of consciousness, or as Harris says in *Tumatumari,* the "translation of the Gorgon."

CHAPTER 5

The Poetics of Identity and Difference: *Black Marsden* and *Concierto barroco*

The ludic conception of the novel, the play of language, form, and ideas in what Harris calls the "Conception of the Game," is the context of the reexamination of writing, history, and cultural identity in Harris's *Black Marsden* (1972) and Carpentier's *Concierto barroco* (1974). The ludic elements in these two later novels are humor, parody, and above all the self-referentiality of the texts. Theater and carnival are the common paradigms for Harris's and Carpentier's experiments with novelistic form in the two works. Both writers emphasize the act of writing as improvisation and role playing; but their aim, like that of the carnival masque, is to overthrow all notions of cultural domination in order to achieve an open-ended vision of fiction and reality.

In these two novels the journey is the inverse route of the conquest, the return to the Old World where the protagonists encounter unexpected cultural parallels and arrive at a new understanding of personal identity. *Black Marsden* is the story of Clive Goodrich, a native of South America, who now resides in Scotland after winning a fortune gambling in the football pools. He becomes the wealthy patron of a group of derelict artists who turn his home into a *"tabula rasa"* theater, which is related to Harris's concept of art as the transformation of a blank tablet or the void. Carpentier's novel, which takes place in both the eighteenth and twentieth centuries, relates the journey of a wealthy Mexican and his Cuban servant to Europe, where they have an extraordinary meeting with the baroque composers Vivaldi, Scarlatti, and Handel. This cross-cultural encounter is a comedy of erroneous perceptions in which the Americans witness the transformation of their history into a melodramatic opera.

The cross-cultural landscape in *Black Marsden* is Scotland and South America. Harris suggests an affinity between Scottish and American culture as well as his own concept of the novel when he cites Kurt Wittig on Scottish literary tradition as one of "duality" and "split personality" with a marked tendency toward subjectivity:

> From the beginning, (this) poetry showed a combination of two or more seemingly irreconcilable qualities: of high pathos and everyday realism, of stark tragedy and grim humour, of high seriousness and grotesquerie, of tenderness and sarcasm. . . . This emotional and intellectual dualism—the "Caledonian Antisyzygy"—*may* possibly have been reinforced by the schizophrenic tendencies of a nation which came to use one language to express thought, another to express feeling. . . . At any rate, the problem of a strangely subjective vision of reality is dominant.[1]

The duality and subjective vision associated with the Caledonian Antisyzygy are also the prevailing characteristics of Harris's exploration of the poetics of difference and identity in *Black Marsden*.

Fiction and reality are interchangeable in this novel. Clive Goodrich both lives and writes his adventure. The episodic structure of the text consists of a series of anecdotes and dialogues that the protagonist himself describes as "rambling absurd improvisation" (17). Since the wealthy Goodrich is at leisure to indulge his passion for walking around, the novel is composed of chance encounters and random reflections triggered by his observations of place. He compares the "naive and complex features" of the legends associated with the kings and ancient ruins of pre-Renaissance Scotland to those of pre-

130

Columbian America (11). Goodrich writes his impressions in a diary, which he continually revises; and since everything is "grist for his mill," he refers to himself as a "miser of infinity" (37).

On one of his many excursions, he finds Doctor Black Marsden— clown, conjurer, and hypnotist extraordinary—half-frozen among the ruins of Dunfermline Abbey in the county of Fife. He reminds Goodrich of the fabled magicians who were said to have slept in ice or snow. Goodrich arouses Marsden from his half-frozen state and instantly enters a strange alliance with him that transforms his daily existence into a "condition of marvel" (12). The magician's arousal also provides the necessary conditions for the marvelous in the text we read: the release of the inner forces of psyche as well as the creative powers of the imagination.[2]

The principal symbol of duality and the transformative power of the imagination in *Black Marsden* is the Gorgon figure, now associated with art, "the open-ended mystery of beauty—flesh into stone or vice versa" (13). In addition to Gorgon, Marsden will reveal to Goodrich the mysteries of Knife, who (like life and death) is "both straight and twisted," and Harp, the bent "vibrating touchstone" of the inner self. Goodrich invites Doctor Marsden to stay at his home in Edinburgh, and it is there that the derelict-magician introduces him to his friends Jennifer Gorgon, a London nightclub singer; Knife, a beggar; and Harp, a frustrated musician. These down-and-out characters make up Marsden's "open-ended circus of reality." Each acts as an agent of consciousness in Clive Goodrich's real and imaginary adventure.

Marsden, the magician, is adept at "divine cross-lateral jokes (left-hand telepathy)" (19). His presence provokes a series of dreams and fantasies in Goodrich's imagination. One such dream is the "camera" episode. Shortly after the arrival of Jennifer, the "Gorgon Spring," Goodrich learns that Marsden has been taking pictures with his "flash bulb camera." That evening he lies in bed obsessed by his aversion to cameras: "Half-waking, half-sleeping questions robed in abstract concreteness or concrete abstractness (it was difficult to tell which) began to plague my mind. Who or what was this camera?" (18). He then has a dream about Marsden dressed up in a camera costume. The derelict-magician slides along the floor begging for money, quoting Robert Burns, and spouting terse bits of wisdom: "The Church like the Poor like Art is always with us" (21). Then with a clap of his hands, he produces Jennifer "naked as a sea-shell" and Knife "sharp as bone or sin" from beneath the black cloth of his costume. Suddenly Knife slashes the camera, leaving Marsden as naked as Jennifer. Goodrich is outraged by the "impropriety" of this scene, but Marsden responds: "Naked propriety. . . . I am inventing a new style for both pulpit and theatre. She is our divided enchantress. Moral pence in church or bedroom. And a million dirt-cheap in the theatre of the world. We have created an ambiguity. And out of that ambiguity is born the Knife of humanity" (22).

For Harris, the camera, like conventional realism, gives a one-dimensional picture of reality that fails to present the ambiguity and complexity of human experience. In this sense the "realism" of the camera is *misrepresentation* masquerading as the real, which he associates with dogma and tyranny. Freedom, on the other hand, as Goodrich says in his diary, is "the unravelling of self-portraits and self-deceptions" (24), the "naked propriety" or truth that dogmatic realism would cover up.

According to Goodrich, the twentieth-century quest for freedom through technology is the "naked bias" that perpetuates the saying, *"never let your right hand know what your left hand is doing"* (19). He writes a sketch of what he calls the "comedy of Freedom," a dialogue between the "realistic" right hand and the "visionary" left hand.[3] The art of the imagination, unlike the one-dimensionality of the camera, is "a sleeping ambidextrous Queen (uniquely gifted, not double-dealing or slippery)" (19), which in Harris's view is the only salvation from catastrophe.

In *Black Marsden*, the derelict-magician and his associates are reifications of Harris's ideas about the nature of fiction and reality in the novel. As Maes-Jelinek points out, this is "partly a novel of ideas but one in which ideas are also concretized into characters or incidents."[4] Another example of the self-referential emphasis of the text is the Tabula Rasa Global Theatre. Marsden sets up the *tabula rasa* theater to produce a play, which will be a new version of the story of John the Baptist; Knife will play the role of a beggar and Jennifer that of a "thoroughly virtuous" Salome. When Goodrich objects to this interpretation as a "violation of the part," Jennifer responds mimicking Marsden: " 'What is virtue? Virtue is a succession of violations towards the seat of love—towards the possession of head or heart. Virtue is a cruel insistence on a property of reality' " (34).

Marsden's *tabula rasa* drama is the "play within a play which repudiates the play of bias" (57). Like the novel, its aim is to break down the barriers of consciousness and create an open vision of reality. Both the novel and Marsden's theatrical production share the spatial properties of Goodrich's frequent dreams, "in that a motif appears and asserts itself in the dream to define and redefine the nature of community beyond conformity to a status of hubris. Acquittal, therefore, from hubris is nothing more than the revitalized life of the imagination to re-assess blocked perspectives and to begin to digest as well as liberate contrasting figures" (54).

Marsden and his associates are also actors (the liberating agents of illumination) in Clive Goodrich's "private theatre" (104). When Harp, the musician, arrives from Canada, Goodrich takes an immediate liking to him. Harp's passion is "mopping-up as well as preserving and screening relations within the ghostly family of man" (46). He is the medium through whom Goodrich is able to experience the correspondence between seemingly unrelated events. When Goodrich tells him that he feels he has known him since "the beginning of time," Harp suggests that they may indeed be related. They are all members of the "commonwealth of man sponsored by ancient Marsden" (47).

Harp tells Goodrich the story of his father John Hornby, who died in the same year and on the same day as the famous Arctic explorer who also bore that name. Harp's goal in life has been to "bridge the distance between two legends—the famous Hornby and the obscure Hornby" (45). As Goodrich listens to his story, Harp ventures into the "Arctic night" of memory:

> He stood upon the very rim of ghostland—one collective foot already in the grave, one legendary cabin already in the sky. Thus as he began to ascend and descend Sky and Creek he became aware that there were two Hornbys projected from him into the cosmos. One was a man drawn out of the hat of millions, so steeped in extremity and danger beyond humanity's lot as to become a private body in the stars, quint-

essential solitariness, Arctic legend of soul. The other was a man standing in the boot of millions so benumbed by humanity's lot as to die
unsung, unheralded, Arctic function of non-memory, non-soul. (49)

In his role as agent of correspondence, Harp is the link between
memory and nonmemory. Goodrich soon discovers the nature of
Harp's role and the strange bond between them, when he takes one of
his favorite walks by the waterside. The open sky and sea of the
Edinburgh landscape merge with memories of his childhood in South
America:

> The blue, green waves curled into animated frescoes of memory that
> seemed to reach towards Harp's horizons and lakes across the Atlantic:
> to reach farther south into the South Americas—South American
> savannahs pasted upon the globe like an abstract realm within fiery
> longitudes. . . .
> All these vistas seemed to curl and uncurl now into ebbing and
> flowing waves and tides. The sea of the sky reached everywhere, spires
> and rocks seemed equally fraught with energies that shot upwards but
> witnessed to an inherent spatial design, geology of psyche. (62)

Goodrich was five years old when his stepfather Rigby, "a tempera-
mental Scot," disappeared in the jungles of Brazil. He is struck by the
coincidence that linked the fate of his stepfather to that of Harp's
father, John Hornby: "Hornby and Rigby Ltd. Goodrich could not
help marvelling in himself as he stared into the distant Water of Leith.
Life was stranger than property. His stepfather Rigby had vanished in
Brazil the very year, the very day Hornby and Hornby had established a pattern of legend in the Arctic. It was a judgment and equally
acquittal of intuitive spaces knitted into the globe. It was an intimate
parallel, Pole and Equator" (65).

The juxtaposition of fire and ice in their fathers' "muse of adventure" is related to the *tabula rasa* drama of conception through which
the transformation of contrasting elements is achieved. Goodrich had
already sensed this relationship when he wrote in his "diary of infinity" that "one lived many lives, died many deaths through others.
There was a renascence or flowering, or a deeper accent of eclipse
upon buried personalities—actors in a tabula rasa drama—in every encounter one enjoyed or endured. Something died. Something

was born. Each element of participation carried within it new and undreamt-of senses of constellations" (64).

After Harp, the "vibrating touchstone" of correspondences, provokes the memory of his past, Goodrich attempts to "revisualize (and revise) his journey across Namless," the country in South America where he was born. Brown Knife, as opposed to White or Black Knife,[5] serves as the guide and interpreter who drives him across Namless in a rickety taxi. Goodrich left Namless when he was six or seven years old after the disappearance of his stepfather in the jungles of Brazil. Namless has changed so much that it seems like a different country; there are signs of abandonment everywhere. A revolution of sorts has taken place as a result of a popular uprising that began with demands for higher wages, better housing, and an end to discrimination. The movement was co-opted, however, when the Authorities sent a Director-General of Cosmic Theatre—instead of troops—to rule over Namless. All the demands were granted, and in the process the country was turned into a totalitarian desert, the "double-cross" of politics.

In his journey across Namless with Knife, Goodrich notices a strange figure lurking in the background. Like Knife he is one of the Director-General's intelligence agents whose mutilated body turns up later in the bushes alongside the road. Knife speculates that perhaps the agent betrayed some "secret orchestra or revolutionary *avant-garde*" (87). Goodrich senses something familiar about the murdered intelligence officer: "something Marsdenish (the shadow of Marsden stretching into the past and into the future of Namless Theatre)" (86). He wonders whether the agent had been caught in a conflict between a "*conscious* mission to rationalize" the totalitarian control over Namless and "a *subconscious* mission to fail," a paradoxical phenomenon of reversal that is related to the concept of the *tabula rasa* comedy (89–90).

On his second day across Namless, Goodrich rebels against Knife's attempt to draw him into the Director-General's "guerrilla theatre" by refusing to accept his authoritarian control.[6] With this refusal, he successfully passes the first trial of his journey. The second comes one evening toward the end of the journey when he hears the plaintive sound of bagpipes rising across the Basin of Namless. Goodrich recalls the Scottish legend of a piper who sacrificed his life to save his master from an ambush by sending out a warning on his bagpipe. Knife claims that in Namless the "Piper's Warning" has been given a new meaning; now it is a signal to go forward rather than turn back, a signal of assurance and safety. Goodrich is skeptical, however, and senses that the music is a warning from Marsden's dead agent. He rejects the new interpretation of the signal, refuses to go forward, and thus brings an end to Knife's role as guide in the journey across Namless.

In this real and imaginary journey, Clive Goodrich reaches back into "the slate of childhood" and emerges with a strange sense of "denuded namelessness" (94). Yet his refusal to submit to Knife's control and his decision to abandon the journey enables him to assume a new, more powerful role in his relationship with Marsden, the director of the *tabula rasa* theater. When he returns to Edinburgh, Goodrich agrees to allow Jennifer Gorgon, who has become pregnant by one of her many lovers, to live in his home. He recognizes a seemingly irrational connection between his acceptance of this new alliance with Jennifer and his decision to abandon the journey across Namless:

> And he felt in his denuded state or shadow against the wall a new tide or re-creative *decision* at the heart of a crowded world. It was a strange realization, a chastening realization, in spite of apparent intoxication: chastening in that he saw himself now in line with both the pale rider in the Royal Mile and the out-of-doors mechanic who had been Jennifer's companions over the past months. He now, as her third potential consort, saw himself equally riddled with the malaise of the twentieth century—with a bankruptcy of authority. And yet in clinging to the annunciation of decision which he made at the door of death, he was beginning to relate himself differently both to the dreadful vacuum of his age and to the implacable biases underlying that age—biased flesh-and-blood, biased creeds, biased refuge of wealth. (99)

As a result of the "re-creative" decision he made on the road to Namless and his pact with Jennifer, Goodrich begins to assert his own authority—both as author of his own consciousness and as author of the *tabula rasa* drama (the play of art and imagination) that takes place in his home. He and Marsden are now "on equal footing in a post-hypnotic threshold to life"; and at their next meeting, the formerly all-powerful director of mind and art appears "drained of some measure of diabolic self-assurance, depleted of an omniscient function" (100).

Now that Goodrich has begun to resent Marsden's control, he feels that it is time to give up his "marvellous discipline in invisibility" (105) and decides to change his shabby, unfashionable clothes for a flashier appearance in order to express his new relationship with Gorgon, the none too virtuous agent of creative transformation. When he appears in his new clothes, Marsden and Jennifer are astonished by his metamorphosis, and Goodrich detects a hint of disapproval that "the world's guinea pig . . . should turn peacock, a usurper of fire, of privileges" (108). But Marsden's authority is not so easily challenged, and besides he is an expert at co-optation. Jennifer has confessed everything and he approves of their plan. Outraged by this betrayal of trust, Goodrich orders them both to leave. He then realizes that Marsden looked like Jennifer's other lovers and had come close to acquiring yet another face—"*his* face."

Goodrich resists the threat of losing his identity to Marsden, as he did in the journey across Namless; but despite this newly found "inner fire of resolution," he is left feeling alone, "utterly alone, as upon a post-hypnotic threshold at the heart of one of the oldest cities of Europe" (111). For Harris, a condition of exile (utter solitude) is the necessary paradox of freedom. The "magical commonwealth" is only possible in subjective vision and the creative imagination. In *Black Marsden*, Harris extols the nameless "I," which like art is a *tabula rasa*, a blank slate on which the imagination inscribes an original vision beyond historical biases of race, ideology, and power.

The dualism of language, emotion, and thought is the basis of Harris's improvisational aesthetics in the *tabula rasa* comedy, the play within the play of his ludic discourse. A similar process of duality and improvisation operates in Alejo Carpentier's *Concierto barroco*, where the heterogeneous, contrasting elements of baroque art and jazz are the inspiration for the author's experiments with novelistic form. In *Concierto barroco*, Carpentier returns to the eighteenth century, but the action of the novel projects into the early twentieth century; thus he sets up a parallel between the exuberant spirit of the late baroque period and the jazz age.

Reversing the steps of the conquest, a wealthy Mexican and his Cuban servant Filomeno travel from the Americas to Europe. The relationship between El Amo, the master, and Filomeno is similar to that of Lenormand de Mezy and Ti Noel in *El reino de este mundo;* their commentaries and responses to the experience of the journey serve as *contrapunteo mental* (ideological counterpoint) between two aspects of American cultural awareness, including its racial and class dimensions. El Amo, born in the New World but the son of a Spaniard, is a somewhat pretentious *hombre culto* with a confused sense of cultural identity; whereas Filomeno, of African descent, is a sensible but irreverent musician who is proud of his cultural heritage. The Mexican's journey to Europe in the eighteenth century suggests the expatriate experience of numerous New World intellectuals in the 1920s and 1930s, who must leave home in order to discover a sense of their own identity. This theme is dealt with much less seriously in *Concierto barroco*, however, than in Carpentier's earlier works. The cultural emphasis in this later novel is on the author's concept of the baroque and the universality of the mythic or creative imagination.

The ludic conception of the novel is announced in the biblical epigraph from Psalm 81, which signals the beginning of the author's "baroque" concert. In the opening chapter we are introduced to the wealthy Mexican who is packing his belongings for the long journey to the Old World. Carpentier's description of the Mexican's luxurious home, laden with silver, including "a silver chamber pot, the bottom decorated with a roguish silver eye soon blinded by the foam which, reflecting the silver so intensely, ultimately seemed silvered itself,"[7] is a parody of the descriptive detail of his own baroque style. The play on words and ribald sense of humor with which El Amo and his home are portrayed prepare us for a different approach to the themes dealt with in earlier novels: the quest for origins, the notion of cultural *mestizaje*, and the relationship between writing and history.

The juxtaposition of Old and New world culture and the theme of the conquest is presented in a painting that hangs in the reception hall of the Mexican's Coyoacán mansion. In a fanciful rendition of the "most transcendent event in the country's history," a European artist brings together the major historical figures of the conquest:

> Montezuma was portrayed as part Roman and part Aztec—a Caesar with quetzal-feather headdress seated on a throne, its style a hybrid of Vatican and Tarascan Indian—beneath a canopy held aloft between two halberds, a vague-looking Cuauhtemoc with the face of a young Telemachus, eyes slightly almond-shaped, standing beside him. Before him, Hernán Cortés, a velvet hat on his head, sword in his belt— arrogant boot bestriding the first step of the imperial throne—was frozen in a dramatic tableau of the Conquest. Behind, Friar Bartolomé de Olmedo in the habit of the Mercerderian Order, brandishing a crucifix with a gesture betokening scant friendliness, and Doña Marina, with sandals and Yucatecan *huipil*, arms outstretched in dumb show of intercession, apparently interpreting to the lord of Tenochtitlán what the Spaniard had just said. (35–36)

The decidedly European interpretation of the "great event" in the Italianate style of an earlier period that makes the Aztecs look like Romans adorned with quetzal plumes anticipates one of the principal themes of the novel: the problem of cultural perception and the relationship between historical realism and artistic representation.

El Amo leaves the port of Veracruz accompanied by his servant Francisquillo in what must have been the year 1709.[8] When their ship is disabled by a storm, they take refuge in Havana harbor only to find the city besieged by an epidemic of yellow fever (one of Carpentier's favorite signs of doom and disruption). They are forced to stay in a miserable little village outside of the city where within three days Francisquillo succumbs to the fever, leaving El Amo without a servant, a prerequisite for his trip to Europe where he wishes to make *la gran entrada* playing the role of the wealthy *indiano:*[9] "his dream of the figure he would cut wherever he appeared, wealthy, rolling in wealth, with money to burn, he a grandson of those who had set out from Spain—'their bottoms showing through their breeches,' as the saying goes—to seek their fortune in the land of America" (48). His problem is solved when he meets Filomeno, a free black who reads, writes, and plays a "rude" guitar. The Mexican decides that Filomeno will be quite suitable as a servant since it was fashionable for rich gentlemen to have black valets; and besides which "Moors" were reported to be all over Europe, even in Denmark where "queens, as is well known, have their husbands murdered by poisons" (49). As El Amo's comment indicates, there is a constant interplay between fiction and reality throughout the novel. El Amo accepts what he knows about European theater as fact; in his mind there is no separation between fiction and reality.

This notion is repeated in Filomeno's dramatic account of the legendary feats of his great-grandfather Salvador Golomón, protagonist of the first poem of known authorship written in Cuba, *Espejo de la paciencia* (1608) by Silvestre de Balboa.[10] Filomeno proudly recites lines from this poem in which the African slave appears as a heroic figure who defeats the French pirate Gilberto Giron. El Amo compares Filomeno's storytelling to the oral style of the traders recounting the history of Montezuma and Hernán Cortés in the market places of Mexico.

Throughout Filomeno's reenactment of the legend, the Mexican interjects ironic remarks on both the style and content of Filomeno's story, advising him in accordance with the rules of classical rhetoric to avoid unnecessary digressions and to follow a logical order of development: " 'Get on with your story in a straight line, boy,' interrupted the traveler, 'and don't be veering off on tangents and curves; to arrive at the clear truth calls for many proofs and reproofs' " (50). The self-referential commentaries of Carpentier's text not only call attention to the relationship between orality and writing (viewed by the Mexican as problematic) but also the intertextual focus of the novel. As Filomeno's tale illustrates, *Concierto barroco* is composed of stories that are *retold*.[11]

Carpentier's retelling of *Espejo de la paciencia* serves both as a commentary on the black presence in the history and culture of the Americas as well as a reference to the problematics of American literary tradition since its beginnings in the sixteenth century. El Amo, for example, considers Balboa's reference to satyrs and centaurs in the guava trees of Cuba a product of the poet's "excessive imagination." From the perspective of most modern Caribbean and Latin American literary criticism, Balboa would be accused of excessive imitation of European classical models.[12] Filomeno, however, does not doubt that such marvels could exist in Cuba:

[He] never questioned that in these islands supernatural beings, creatures of classical mythology, should have been seen, similar to many of darker complexion that still inhabit the woods, fountains, and caves here—as they have in the far-off indeterminate kingdoms from whence came the forebears of illustrious Salvador, who was, in his way, a sort of Achilles, inasmuch as, for lack of a real Troy and keeping things in due proportion, one can be an Achilles in Bayamo or an Achilles in Coyoacán, commensurably with the magnitude of events. (53–54)

As in the earlier novel, *El reino de este mundo*, the black protagonist of *Concierto barroco* is identified with the folk imagination. And Filomeno, proud of his ancestry, has no trouble appropriating the "universality" of the mythic legacy attributed to the Greeks.

In his dramatic reenactment of his grandfather's legend, the victory celebration that follows the defeat of the French pirate is described as a "universal concert" in which musicians from Spain, the Canary Islands, creoles, *mestizos, naboríes* (Indian servants), and blacks take part. The wealthy Mexican, however, is skeptical about any such mixing of cultures: "—'An impossible harmony! Never could such folly have occurred, for the noble old melodies of the romance and the subtle modulations and variations of good maestros would have married ill with the barbarous racket raised by Negroes when they set to work with their rattles, maracas, and drums. . . . What an infernal cacophony it would have produced and what a great liar that Balboa must have been!' "(55). The "impossible harmony" of Filomeno's concert is, of course, what New World music becomes in all its various forms from the Afro-Cuban *son* to Afro-American jazz.

In the course of the Mexican's journey with Filomeno through Europe, Carpentier reexamines the relationship between the concept of cultural *mestizaje* and artistic expression dealt with in his earlier writings. The two travelers leave Cuba for Spain, but the Mexican's encounter with the exalted homeland of his forefathers and Hernán Cortés is a disappointment compared to what he left behind in the Americas. He decides to cut short his stay and leave immediately for

Italy in order to get there in time for the Carnival of the Epiphany, which would attract people from all over Europe.

Carnival is the world of unrestrained revelry and parody where cultural values and hierarchies of all kind are turned upside down. The bawdy atmosphere of carnival in Venice is therefore the setting for the break with traditional novelistic conventions of time and space in *Concierto barroco*. It is also here in the inverse world of carnival that the Mexican must confront his own cultural identity. Already playing the role of the wealthy *indiano*, the Mexican decides to dress up as Montezuma. He meets a priest to whom he relates the story of the ruler who lost an empire to "a handful of bold Spaniards with the help of an Indian woman who was in love with the chief of the invaders" (70). Impressed by the theatrical possibilities of the Mexican's story about the Aztec emperor, the priest, who turns out to be the composer Antonio Vivaldi, suggests it would be a good subject for an opera. They are then joined by Scarlatti and Handel, who have just returned from the first performance of the latter's *Agrippina*. This extraordinary encounter therefore takes place on 26 December 1709.[13]

After a drunken discussion about art, the Mexican and Filomeno join the three composers for an evening of music at the Ospedale della Pietà, a famous conservatory for orphaned girls where Vivaldi taught. With Handel at the organ, Scarlatti at the harpsichord, and Vivaldi on the violin, seventy young women perform "the most extraordinary *concerto grosso* the centuries could ever have heard—but the centuries remember[ed] nothing" (79). Meanwhile, Filomeno accompanies them by playing percussion rhythms on some pots and pans he found in the kitchen. What ensues is the "impossible harmony" of Carpentier's baroque concert. This eighteenth-century "jam session" combines the heterogeneous mixtures of sounds and improvisation associated with twentieth-century jazz.

After the concert is brought to a close, Filomeno notices a painting that depicts Eve being tempted by the serpent. The image of the serpent reminds him of an African ritual practiced back home. While making a gesture of killing the snake, Filomeno begins singing an Afro-Cuban chant:

—The snake is dead
Ca-la-ba-són,
Son-són.

Ca-la-ba-són.
Son-són.
(82)

Vivaldi responds by giving the Afro-Cuban verse a Latin variation: *Kábala-sum-sum-sum*. The others join them in this exchange between Africa and Europe, dancing around the room in an eighteenth-century version of the *conga:*

> They all fell into line, hands on each other's waists, swaying their hips, forming the most disparate mummers' troupe imaginable. . . .
>
> . . . *Ca-la-ba-són-són*—sang Filomeno, accenting the beat more strongly each time. *Kábala-sum-sum-sum*, replied the Venetian, the Saxon, and the Neapolitan. *Kábala-sum-sum-sum* repeated the others, until exhausted from so much whirling, running up, running down, going in, going out, they returned to the concert hall and collapsed. (83–84)

Filomeno's Afro-Cuban chant sets in motion a "whirlwind" of transformations in which all cultural barriers are temporarily swept away.[14]

After dancing and drinking until dawn, the Mexican and Filomeno leave the Pietà with the three composers for a cemetery where they can have a quiet picnic breakfast away from the carnival uproar in the city. When they get there, Vivaldi returns to the subject of Montezuma and his idea of turning the story into an opera. He compares the Aztec emperor to the king of ancient Persia, Xerxes. Tired of worn-out themes, he thinks Montezuma would provide something new:

> "All the Orpheuses, all the Apollos, the Iphigenias, Didos, and Galateas! It's time to look for new material, different milieus, other countries, whatever . . . to bring Poland, Scotland, Armenia, Tartary to the theater. Other characters: Geneva, Cunegonde, Griselda, Tamerland, or Scanderbeg the Albanian who gave the damnable Turks such a bad time. There's a fresh wind blowing. The public will soon weary of

143

lovelorn shepherds, constant nymphs, sententious rustics, Olympian panderers, laurel wreaths, moth-eaten peplums, and last season's royal robes." (91)

Filomeno suggests what he thinks would surely be a new subject for the European stage—an opera based on the legend of his great-grandfather Salvador Golomón. When the Saxon (Handel) and the Venetian laugh at the idea, even the Mexican takes offense at the Europeans' response. The *indiano* compares Golomon to the fifteenth-century Slavic hero Scanderbeg: " 'That doesn't sound so farfetched to me. Salvador Golomón fought for his faith against its enemies, the Huguenots, just as Scanderbeg fought for his. If a criollo of ours seems like a savage to you, the same could be said of one of those big Slavs out there' " (91–92).

Carpentier uses the remainder of their graveside discussion to poke fun at cultural prejudices and ignorance. There are whimsical commentaries about Moors in Venice, Gothic queens, the bizarre behavior of Scandinavian princes who play with skeletons, and bad English taste in drama. The boisterous exchange is full of puns and anachronistic references to railroads, Barnum and Bailey, Richard Wagner, and Igor Stravinsky. One such literary gag is Filomeno's trumpet solo in pure Dixieland style, which is greeted with loud protests by the others:

> And all at once, he reached for his cloak rolled up beside the provender and drew out the mysterious object given him "for remembrance"— as he had said—by Catterina del cornetto: It was a gleaming trumpet . . . which he immediately raised to his lips, tested his embouchure, then launched into a series of blares, flutters, glissandos, and shrill whines that evoked vigorous protests from the others, for had they not come there in search of tranquility, to escape the carnival street musicians and, besides, this was not music and, even if it might possibly be construed as such, totally inappropriate in a cemetery, out of respect for the dead lying in peace under their solemn gravestone slabs. (96)

Filomeno's music is of course no more discordant than the jam session at the Ospedale della Pietà, and the Europeans' negative response to it contradicts their own claims to "modernity" and innovation. This episode therefore underscores the relativity of cultural values and prepares the way for a fuller discussion of the relationship between cultural perception and artistic representation when Vivaldi carries out his plan to turn the story of Montezuma into an opera.

The following episode supposedly takes place the day after the Carnival celebrations of the evening of 26 December 1709. In fact, however, the Mexican is awakened by Filomeno from a deep sleep some twenty-four years later in the fall of 1733 on the day of the first performance of Vivaldi's *Montezuma*. They attend a rehearsal of the new opera, for which the Mexican has contributed his Montezuma costume. Vivaldi's operatic version of the conquest is reminiscent of the painting in his house in Coyoacan, but even less faithful to reality. The *indiano* is deeply disturbed by Vivaldi's artistic adaptations: the Mexican scenery looks too much like Venice, Montezuma's empress is a cross between Semiramis and a Titian lady, Teutile—the leader of Montezuma's armies—is transformed into a woman, and La Malinche, the conquistador's Indian interpreter and lover, is eliminated altogether since no Italian opera singer would ever accept such a part.

The Mexican is enraged by Vivaldi's melodramatic ending in which Hernán Cortés forgives his enemies, and the friendship between Aztecs and Spaniards is celebrated with the marriage of the female Teutile and Ramiro, the younger brother of the Spanish conquistador. When the *indiano* protests against the historical inaccuracies, Vivaldi responds: "Stop giving me that history crap. Poetic illusion is what counts in the theater" (116). Furthermore, according to him, "In America everything is fantastical [*fabuloso*]: tales of El Dorados and Potosís, fabulous cities, talking sponges, sheep with red fleece, Amazons with only one breast, big-eared Incas who eat Jesuits" (117). The composer's response is an ironic inversion of Carpentier's own concept of the marvelous in American reality and repeats what had become the essence of European discourse on the Americas since the arrival of Columbus and the conquistadors.

In the final episode of the novel, the two Americans reflect on the significance of their journey and the relationship between history and fable. Vivaldi's operatic rendition of the conquest forces the Mexican to see himself differently. Although he is the grandson of a Spanish conquistador, while he watched the opera he wanted Montezuma to

145

win out over the arrogance of Hernan Cortes. He now considers himself, as he says, "on the Americans' side, brandishing the same weapons and willing the ruination of those to whom I owe my blood and my name" (122). It seemed that the opera singer dressed up in his borrowed Montezuma costume was playing a role that belonged to him. He suddenly felt out of place, exotic, far from what was truly his; but he realizes that *"it is sometimes necessary to distance yourself from things, to put an ocean in between, in order to get a close look at them"* (123). He then decides to leave Venice and return home that very night, to return to *lo suyo.*[15]

Commenting on the Mexican's response to Vivaldi's opera, Filomeno observes that the purpose of theatrical illusion is "to remove us from where we are and take us to where we can't get to on our own"; to which the Mexican adds, "It also serves us—and this was written by an ancient philosopher—to purge ourselves of anxieties hidden in the deepest, most secret places of the self. . . . On seeing the America contrived by that bad poet Giusti, I no longer felt myself a spectator and became one of the actors" (122). Through illusion and fabrication art, like traditional mythic discourse (and the carnival saturnalia for that matter), is a means of releasing the inner conflicts of the psyche. The two Americans now recognize that the validity of art, like myth, resides not in its absolute fidelity to historical fact but in its ability to transform consciousness.

Referring to Vivaldi's comment that in America everything is fable, the Mexican expresses Carpentier's concept of myth as memories of the future: " 'You mustn't forget that great history feeds on fable. Our world seems like a fable to the people over here because they've lost the sense of the fabulous. They call everything fabulous that is remote, irrational, that belongs to yesterday. . . . They don't understand that the fabulous is in the future. The future is entirely fabulous' " (123). The Mexican's understanding of the relationship between mythic discourse and history recalls Vico's axiom that all "histories have fabulous beginnings" and that myth and fable are forms of poetic divination; that is, creative hypotheses about human history.[16]

Furthermore, the structure of the narrative in *Concierto barroco* imitates the temporal dislocations of mythic discourse: past and present are projected into the future. The final episode of the novel is presented as a direct sequel to the rehearsal of Vivaldi's opera. It actually takes place, however, in two different historical periods—the year Handel produced his most celebrated work, the *Messiah* (1742), and the 1920s. After the *indiano* decides to return home, the narrative suddenly shifts from the mid-eighteenth century to the early twentieth century. The Mexican is now boarding a train, ready to settle down in his Wagons-Lits-Cook compartment. But Filomeno plans to stay another day so that he can attend a concert and then go on to Paris where they will address him as "Monsieur Philomène" rather than just "*el negrito Filomeno*" as they do back home in Havana.[17]

Before parting, Filomeno and the Mexican discuss the need for a revolution to change those old racial prejudices and the trumpet as the instrument of the Apocalypse, the revolutionary End of Time that brings about a new beginning:

> "That's why they blow it so often at the trials on the great Day of Judgment when it comes to settling accounts with sons-of-bitches and snakes-in-the grass," said the black.
> "We won't be seeing the last of those until the end of time," replied the criollo.
> "It's a funny thing," observed Filomeno, "but I always hear about the end of time. Why not talk about the beginning of time?"
> "That would be the Day of Resurrection," answered the criollo.
> "I don't have the time to wait all that time," said the black . . .
> The big hand of the station clock jumped the second separating it from 8 p.m. Almost imperceptibly, the train started to slip into the night. (127)

By presenting this final exchange between the two travelers in the eighth chapter at eight o'clock in the evening, Carpentier once again underscores the spiral-like movement of time and consciousness, as well as the structure of the novel itself.[18]

As the train goes off into the distance, Filomeno turns toward the city lights, and Venice seems to have grown tremendously old. Now it stands as a monument to the passage of time, signaling the age of traveler's checks when journeys no longer have the same prestige as in former times. Filomeno, however, is looking forward to a Louis Armstrong concert that night. For him, the sound of Armstrong's

147

trumpet is "the only thing . . . alive, current, and pointing like an arrow toward the future" (129).

Jazz, like Carpentier's novel, is the terrestrial music that takes the place of the old myths that have been degraded in an age of technological progress and consumerism. Filomeno compares it to the universal music evoked by Balboa in *Espejo de la paciencia* and the baroque jam session at the Ospedale della Pietà. This "new baroque concert" combines the musical traditions of Africa, Europe, and America into an art form associated with the quest for social as well as artistic freedom. As an expression of New World culture, jazz transforms the original clash of cultures into a new beginning. Jazz is Carpentier's metaphor for the dialectics of culture, in which the notion of cultural hegemony is overturned, allowing for individual expression within the context of collectivity, his redefinition of universal culture.

The journey in both *Concierto barroco* and *Black Marsden* is a process of duality, inversion, and transformation in which the protagonists confront questions of personal identity and the relationship between art and reality. In the resolution of the Old World/New World dichotomy, however, the South American protagonist of *Black Marsden* remains poised on the threshold of awareness in a state of exile, the nameless void of the *tabula rasa* theater; whereas his counterpart in *Concierto barroco*, the Mexican *indiano*, overcomes the alienation of his divided consciousness and *chooses* the New World tradition of cultural plurality, the "impossible harmony" of the new baroque concert or jazz. Furthermore, the Mexican's alter ego Filomeno (like Ti Noel in *El reino de este mundo*) plays an important role in perpetuating the revolutionary content of the mythic imagination. For even in the twentieth century when the vitality of the old myths is undermined by modern science and commerce, he sees the creation of new mythic forms projected into the future.

Conclusion

The dual process of naming and unnaming is where myth and history intersect in the novels of Carpentier, Harris, and Glissant. Each of these writers recreates a history that has been perceived as absence or catastrophe in order to give it new meaning. Their aim is to transform the void of historical rupture and fragmentation into an open-ended vision of possibility. In this sense, their novels, like myth, are memories of the future.

In their innovative experiments with myth, fable, and legend, these writers express a common concern for new approaches to Caribbean history and culture. Although concrete historical experience informs the mythic elements in their novels and while they often seem to use the same language, to paraphrase Esteban in *El siglo de las luces,* their concepts of myth and history differ in some fundamental ways. For Carpentier there is a dynamic interaction between the mythic and historical imagination. In his novels, myth functions as a motivating force in bringing about historical change. Thus the ancient myths of Africa inspire the slave rebellions in *El reino de este mundo* in much the same way as social ideals (the secular myth of the promised land) inspire eighteenth- and nineteenth-century revolutions in *El siglo de las luces*.

Despite Glissant's distrust of what he considers the scriptural transcendence implied in archetypal myth, his concept of writing as "creative hypothesis" is analogous to the problem-reflecting function of myth. In *Quatrième* and *La case* he transforms the myth of origins into speculative inquiries about the nature of historical experience in colonial Martinique. His plantation stories become revolutionary myths of the ceaseless struggle to find an opening through the void of historical memory and to name one's own place in the world.

Wilson Harris, on the other hand, always establishes a negative correlation between myth and history in his fiction. Although he maintains that history—like the "perspective of the Gorgon"—is capable of creative transformation, in his novels the subjective, intuitive vision of myth functions in opposition to any material vision of time. Since he has little faith in the possibility of human progress within the framework of any existing social system, for him history is still the nightmare from which Caribbean writers are trying to awake. His strategy is therefore to *subvert* the role of history, which he considers all too dominant in Caribbean fiction, by subordinating it to that of the mythic imagination.

The differences in their approaches to historical representation in the novel ultimately reflect radically different ideologies about the role of the writer and the relationship between art and society. Harris advocates an open-ended vision of reality in which the unpredictability of human experience is paramount. Like other modern writers, he therefore rejects traditional realism in the novel because he believes it "fossilizes" circumstances and relationships. On these same grounds, he rejects existing models of social change since, as he sees it, they perpetuate the victor/victim polarizations of the conquest. Thus in his novels, active participation in the historical process always ends in the double cross of politics. Harris maintains that the role of the writer is to undermine the "mechanical platforms of the world" (*Tradition* 9); his foremost commitment is therefore to promote a vision of the complexity of life in all its contradictions. Although all his novels express the need for change, it is only realized, however, in individual consciousness and art.

While Carpentier and Glissant also reject oversimplifications of Caribbean history and culture, they assert the artist's personal commitment to political and social change. Carpentier's novels tend to focus on collective struggles in which heroism and triumph are possible in spite of conflict and betrayal. For Carpentier, historical conflict gives rise to social change in much the same way as the conflicting elements of New World culture give rise to the symbiotic process of transformation in art (the underlying poetics of marvelous realism). From the perspective of still-colonized Martinique, Glissant's narratives of resistance all point to the need for a liberation of consciousness that ultimately can only take place beyond the text in the realm of political action. The desire for an independent Martinique, an island engaged in the same struggle for nationhood as the other islands of the Caribbean, however problematic that might be, is very much a part of his fictional discourse.

Despite their differences, these writers have sought a redefinition of the poetics of the novel in the context of New World history and culture. They consider the process of creolization that took place in the Caribbean to be a manifestation of the dialectics of identity and difference that informs their own cross-cultural poetics. The quest for origins in their novels does not reestablish the mythical Golden Age before conquest and slavery. Instead it leads to affirmation of the creative potential of the future in the roots of the past. Their fiction offers a new vision of community based on the acceptance of cultural diversity in an interdependent world. But as Clive Goodrich says in *Black Marsden:* "It is one thing to evoke a magical commonwealth (all races, all times). It's another thing to prove it" (46).

The historical legacy of colonialism—economic exploitation, racial conflict, and ideological divergence—continues to undermine the possibility of cross-cultural unity among the heterogeneous peoples of the Caribbean. From the 1920s to the 1940s, writers such as Aimé Césaire and Jacques Roumain, Nicolás Guillén and Alejo Carpentier, played a major role in developing a pan-Caribbean cultural awareness. Albeit from differing political and literary perspectives, a

151

later generation of writers such as Edouard Glissant, Maryse Condé, Simone Schwarz-Bart, Wilson Harris, George Lamming, Edward Brathwaite, and Derek Walcott have all promoted the notion of a cultural dialogue among the peoples of the Caribbean.

The decline of colonialism and the achievement of independence in most of the islands by the late 1960s gave rise to a complex, difficult process of economic and cultural decolonization. These and other sociopolitical factors, including the impact of the Cuban Revolution, have contributed to the conscious efforts of Caribbean artists and intellectuals to explore the common historical and cultural legacy of the region as a whole. This movement led to the establishment of the Caribbean Festival of the Arts (Carifesta) in 1972, which was held for the first time in Georgetown, Guyana, with representatives from all the language areas of the Caribbean. Since that time the nations of the Caribbean have undergone many political alliances and disaffections, but among the major writers of the Caribbean the ideal of a cross-cultural dialogue persists.

Notes

Introduction

1. Roberto González Echevarría, *Alejo Carpentier: The Pilgrim at Home* (Ithaca, N.Y.: Cornell University Press, 1977), p. 25.

2. Wilson Harris, "History, Fable and Myth in the Caribbean and Guianas," *Caribbean Quarterly* 16 (June 1970): 6, 21.

3. For Vico the study of myth and language was a method of historical investigation; he maintained that myth and fables were the "first histories of the gentile nations" and that poets were the first historians. See *The New Science of Giambattista Vico*, rev. trans. of the 3d ed. (1744) by Thomas Goddard Bergin and Max Harold Fisch (Ithaca, N.Y.: Cornell University Press, 1968), pp. 33, 105.

4. Claude Lévi-Strauss, "The Science of the Concrete," *The Savage Mind* (Chicago: University of Chicago Press, 1966), pp. 1–33.

5. In "Rethinking Myth," Okpewho writes: "Myth is not really a particular type of tale, as so many scholars . . . have pointed out in their generic definitions; nor is it the spoken counterpart of enacted sequences in ritual, as scholars like Jane Harrison would have it. It is simply that quality of fancy which informs the creative or configurative power of the human mind in varying degrees of intensity; in that sense we are free to call any narrative of the oral tradition myth—so long as it lays emphasis on fanciful idea" (*African*

Literature Today 11 [1980]: 19). Okpewho's emphasis on "fanciful play" is related to his interest in the aesthetic and performance aspects of oral traditions, which is the subject of his study *The Epic in Africa* (New York: Columbia University Press, 1979).

6. G. S. Kirk, *Myth: Its Meaning and Functions in Ancient and Other Cultures* (London: Cambridge University Press; Berkeley: University of California Press, 1970), p. 258. Kirk's concept of the speculative myth is related to Claude Lévi-Strauss's idea that the function of myth is to "mediate" contradictions, but he rejects the general application of this theory to all myth. Kirk's position is that "there is no one definition of myth, no Platonic form of a myth against which all actual instances can be measured. Myths . . . differ enormously in their morphology and their social function" (p. 7). In a more recent study, applying structuralist and poststructuralist theories of language, myth, and psychology, Eric Gould argues that the problem-solving function of myth is a fundamental aspect of mythopoesis in modern literature (see *Mythical Intentions in Modern Literature* [Princeton: Princeton University Press, 1981]).

7. Daniel-Henri Pageaux, *"El Reino de este mundo* ou les chemins de l'utopie," *Komparatistische Hefte* (University of Bayreuth) 9/10 (1984): 60. "Le mythe est Histoire et pas seulement histoire. Il est l'Histoire d'un groupe, d'une communauté, d'un ensemble culturel. Il se nourrit de l'Histoire du groupe. . . . mais il est toujours réexplication de l'Histoire. En ce sens, le mythe redouble toujours l'Histoire, parce qu'il n'apparaît historiquement que comme Histoire compensatrice. C'est le manque (réel ou tenu pour tel) de certaines réalités ou données historiques qui explique comment le mythe apparaît, se dit et s'écrit comme Histoire seconde. Cette définition . . . permet de voir l'histoire/Histoire mythiques comme une donnée compensatrice face à une situation tenue pour frustrante, face à une situation de souffrance, de manque." All translations are mine unless otherwise indicated.

8. Edouard Glissant, *Le discours antillais* (Paris: Seuil, 1981), pp. 252–53. See also Frantz Fanon's critique of the Jungian archetype and universalizing theories of culture in *Black Skin, White Masks* (New York: Grove Press, 1967), pp. 187–93. All references to *Le discours antillais* are to the original French edition of Glissant's text, for which I have used my own translations of cited passages. Since the completion of my early work on the present study, Michael Dash has published an English translation of the principal essays in *Discours*, with an excellent introduction to Glissant's work; see *Caribbean Discourse: Selected Essays* (Charlottesville: University Press of Virginia, 1989).

9. Glissant, *Discours antillais*, p. 138. Glissant cites two examples of myth as a "producer" of history: Greek warriors singing the exploits of Achilles on the eve of their victory over the Persians at Marathon in 490 B.C. and the Haitians' use of the tales of Mackandal to spur them on in their victory over Napoleon's troops in 1802.

10. Glissant, *Discours antillais*, pp. 138–39, 151. My translation. "[L]e mythe consacre la parole et la voue par avance au rituel de l'écrit; sur ce plan, le conte procède par accès sacrilèges. Ce qu'il agresse ainsi, c'est d'abord le sacré du signe écrit. Le conte antillais balise une histoire déportée par l'édit et la loi. Il est l'anti-édit et l'anti-loi, c'est-à-dire l'anti-écriture."

11. Wilson Harris, *The Womb of Space: The Cross-Cultural Imagination* (Westport, Conn.: Greenwood Press, 1983), p. 18; and Glissant, *Discours antillais*, pp. 191, 192.

12. Wolfgang Bader, "Poétique antillaise, poétique de la relation—Interview avec Edouard Glissant," *Komparatistische Hefte* (University of Bayreuth) 9/10 (1984): 90.

13. Harris, *Womb of Space*, p. 26.

14. Gordon Rohlehr, "The Problem of the Problem of Form: The Idea of an Aesthetic Continuum and Aesthetic Code-switching in West Indian Literature," *Caribbean Quarterly* 31 (March 1985): 3.

15. Glissant, "Le Roman des Amériques," *Discours antillais*, pp. 255–56.

16. Harris, "History, Fable and Myth," p. 6.

1 / *Lo real maravilloso* in Caribbean Fiction

1. Jacques Stéphen Alexis, "Du réalisme merveilleux des Haïtiens," *Présence Africaine* 8–10 (June–November 1956): 263. "L'art haïtien présente en effet le réel avec son cortège d'étrange, de fantastique, de rêve, de demi-jour, de mystère et de merveilleux. . . . notre art à nous tend à la plus exacte représentation sensuelle de la réalité, à l'intuition créatrice, au caractère, à la puissance expressive. Cet art ne recule pas devant la difformité, le choquant, le contraste violent, devant l'antithèse en tant que moyen d'émotion et d'investigation esthétique . . . il aboutit à un nouvel équilibre, plus contrasté, à une composition aussi harmonieuse dans son contradictoire, à une grâce toute intérieure née du singulier et de l'antithétique." (All translations of cited passages from the text of Alexis's speech are mine.)

2. Alexis, "Du réalisme merveilleux," pp. 263, 264.

3. Alexis, "Du réalisme merveilleux," p. 267: "Qu'est-ce donc que le Merveilleux sinon l'imagerie dans laquelle un peuple enveloppe son expérience, reflète sa conception du monde. . . . Le Merveilleux implique certes la naïveté, l'empirisme sinon le mysticisme, mais la preuve a été faite qu'on peut y envelopper autre chose. . . . n'est-ce pas le rêve cosmique d'abondance et de fraternité de ce peuple qui souffre toujours de la faim et du dénuement?"

4. Alexis, "Du réalisme merveilleux," pp. 250–51: "La culture est une donnée qui embrasse toute la vie d'un peuple, depuis les débuts de sa formation, sa constitution progressive, jusqu'à son organisation moderne: la culture est un devenir incessant dont les origines se perdent dans la nuit des temps, et dont les perspectives s'estompent dans le brouillard de l'avenir."

5. Alexis, "Du réalisme merveilleux," p. 267.

6. Translated and cited by Michael Dash from *Reflets d'Haiti*, 21 January 1956, no. 16 in "Jacques Stéphen Alexis," *Black Images* 3 (1975): 47.

7. Alexis, "Du réalisme merveilleux," pp. 260–61, 264.

8. Alexis, "Du réalisme merveilleux," pp. 259–60, 263.

9. See Dash, "Marvelous Realism—The Way Out of Negritude," *Black Images* 3, no. 1 (January 1974): 80–95.

10. Alexis, "Du réalisme merveilleux," p. 258: "La manière dont ils se sont aidés pour conquérir leur indépendance respective, l'aide de Dessalines et de Pétion au général Mexicain Mina, à Miranda, à Bolivar, les volontaires haïtiens qui ont versé leur sang sur les terres latino-américaines, tout cela crée une fraternité qui favorise la confluence culturelle."

11. See Michael Dash, *Literature and Ideology in Haiti, 1915–1961* (Totowa, N.J.: Barnes and Noble, 1981), pp. 182–84, and Carolyn Fowler, *A Knot in the Thread: The Life and Works of Jacques Roumain* (Washington, D.C.: Howard University Press, 1980).

12. Dash, "Jacques Stéphen Alexis," pp. 44–45.

13. See Alexis, "Du rèalisme merveilleux," pp. 264–71. Michael Dash points to Carpentier as the probable source of Alexis's use of the term in *Literature and Ideology*, pp. 195–96.

14. Lamming, *The Pleasures of Exile* (1960; London and New York: Allison & Busby, 1984), p. 9.

15. See Herbert S. Gershman, *The Surrealist Revolution in France* (Ann Arbor: University of Michigan Press, 1974), pp. 147, 231.

16. Carpentier, Prólogo, *El reino de este mundo*, with "Estudio preliminar" by Florinda Friedmann de Goldberg, (Barcelona: EDHASA, 1980), p. 51: "Después de sentir el nada mentido sortilegio de las tierras de Haití, de haber hallado advertencias mágicas en los caminos rojos de la Meseta Central, de haber oído los tambores del Petro y del Rada, me vi llevado a acercar la maravillosa realidad recién vivida a la agotante pretensión de suscitar lo maravilloso que caracterizó cierta literatura de estos últimos treinta años." Prólogo, pp. 55–56: "Se encuentra a cada paso en las vidas de hombres que inscribieron fechas en la historia del Continente. . . . desde los buscadores de la Fuente de la Eterna Juventud, de la áurea ciudad de Manoa, hasta ciertos rebeldes de la primera hora o ciertos héroes modernos de nuestras guerras de independencia. . . . Y es que, por la virginidad del paisaje, por la formación, por la ontología, por la Revelación que constituyó su reciente descubrimiento, por los fecundos mestizajes que propició, América esta muy lejos de haber agotado su caudal de mitologías." (The translations of citations from the prologue are mine.)

17. See Alexis's description of Haitian art, "Du réalisme merveilleux," p. 263. Also Irlemar Chiampi refers to this as the principle of "non-disjunction" inherent in the ideology and poetics of marvelous realism in *O*

realismo maravilhoso: forma e ideologia no romance hispano-americano (São Paulo: Editora Perspectiva, 1980), pp. 157–58.

18. There have been various studies on Carpentier's relationship to the surrealists. See for example: Klaus Müller-Bergh, "Corrientes vanguardistas y surrealismo en la obra de Alejo Carpentier," and Emir Rodríguez Monegal, "Lo real y lo maravilloso en *El reino de este mundo*," *Asedios a Alejo Carpentier*, ed. Müller-Bergh (Santiago de Chile: Editorial Universitaria, 1972), pp. 13–38, 101–32; also Rodríguez Monegal, "La narrativa hispanoamericana. Hacia una nueva 'poética,'" *Teoría de la novela*, ed. Santos Sanz Villanueva y Carlos J. Barbachano (Madrid: Sociedad General Española, 1976), pp. 171–206, and González Echevarría, *The Pilgrim*, pp. 121–27.

19. Carpentier, "La cultura de los pueblos que habitan en las tierras del Mar Caribe," *Casa de las Américas* (La Habana) 20 (January–February 1980):4; repr. in *La novela latinoamericana en vísperas de un nuevo siglo y otros ensayos* (Mexico: Siglo Veintiuno, 1981), pp. 177–89.

20. Carpentier, *The Lost Steps*, trans. Harriet de Onis (New York: Avon Books, 1979), p. 78; originally published in Spanish as *Los pasos perdidos* (Mexico: EDIAPSA, 1953).

21. Carpentier, "Problemática de la actual novela latinoamericana," *Tientos y diferencias* (1964; Montevideo: Editorial Arca, 1967), pp. 18–19; see also Irlemar Chiampi, *O realismo maravilhoso*, on the theme of cultural *mestizaje* in Latin American discussions of American reality and its relationship to marvelous realism (pp. 125–34). In his most recent collection of essays, *Poétique de la Relation* (Paris: Gallimard, 1990), Edouard Glissant extends the notion of a "naturalized" baroque to include his concept of *la relation*. He maintains that as a global, transhistorical phenomenon, the baroque is more than just an art form; it is a new mode of "being-in-the-world" that asserts the diversity and unpredictability in the interrelationship of cultures ("D'un baroque mondialisé," pp. 91–94).

22. Carpentier, "Problemática," p. 37: "Todo lo que nos define, envuelve y circunda: todo lo que opera con energía de *contexto*—para situarlo en lo universal. . . . Nuestra ceiba, nuestros árboles, vestidos o no de flores, se tienen que hacer universales por la operación de las palabras cabales"; "Problemática," pp. 37–38: "Nuestro arte siempre fue barroco: desde la espléndida escultura precolombina y el de los códices, hasta la mejor novelística actual de América, pasándose por las catedrales y monasterios coloniales de nuestro continente. . . . No temamos, pues, el barroquismo en el estilo, en la visión de los contextos, en la visión de la figura humana enlazada por las enredaderas del verbo."

23. Sypher, *Rococo to Cubism in Art and Literature* (New York: Vintage Books, 1960), p. 20. See also Eric Gould's analysis of the metaphorical nature of myth in *Mythical Intentions*, pp. 44–55, 56–59.

24. See Jonathan Culler's discussion of mythological logic and baroque

imagery in *Structuralist Poetics,* pp. 40–41, 102–3; and Chiampi, *O realismo maravilhoso,* pp. 84–87.

25. Carpentier, "Problemática," *Tientos y diferencias,* pp. 14–15, 18–19, and Culler, *Structuralist Poetics* (Ithaca, N.Y.: Cornell University Press, 1975), p. 103.

26. Glissant, *L'intention poétique* (Paris: Seuil, 1969), p. 137: "L'Occident, dépouillé des tabous dont il s'est paré afin de perpétuer sa domination; voici un monde nouveau, avec ses outrances, ses aspirations, ses valeurs. . . . Mais cette oeuvre est en même temps ouverte sur une expérience commune à des millions d'hommes; car le débat est d'un choc de cultures, et ce qui est joué ici c'est l'avenue possible d'une unité."

27. J. A. George Irish, "Magical Realism: A Search for Caribbean and Latin American Roots," *Revista/Review Interamericana* 4 (Fall 1974): 411–13, 418; originally published in *The Literary Half-Yearly* (West Indies Number) 11 (1970). For the purposes of this study I would like to make a distinction between the term commonly referred to in English as *magical realism* and Carpentier's *lo real maravilloso.* See Chiampi's study of the difference between the two terms, *O real maravilhoso,* pp. 19–39; R. González Echevarría, *The Pilgrim,* pp. 107–29; and Rodríguez Monegal, "La narrativa hispanoamericana," *Teoría de la novela,* pp. 177–228.

28. Irlemar Chiampi, *O real maravilhoso,* pp. 130–31, 133–34.

29. The Caribbean poet and historian Edward Kamau Brathwaite discusses the process of creolization and the need to "see the fragments/whole" in *Contradictory Omens: Cultural Diversity and Integration in the Caribbean* (1974; Kingston: Savacou, 1985). Compare Glissant, "Poétique de la Relation," *Discours antillais,* pp. 189–270, and Harris, *The Womb of Space.*

30. Glissant, *Discours antillais,* pp. 190–92; and "Pour l'opacité," *Poétique de la Relation,* pp. 203–9.

31. See Edmundo Desnoes, "El siglo de las luces," *Homenaje a Alejo Carpentier,* ed. Helmy F. Giacoman (New York: Las Americas, 1970), pp. 303, 312–13; and Jean Franco, *Historia de la literatura hispanoamericana* (Barcelona: Editorial Ariel, 1985), pp. 360–61.

32. Glissant, "Le Roman des Amériques," *Discours antillais,* pp. 254–62; "Le Même et le Divers," *Discours antillais,* p. 192.

33. Glissant, *Discours antillais,* pp. 242, 256.

34. Harris, "History, Fable and Myth," 7–12.

35. Harris, "History, Fable and Myth," pp. 9–10, 15.

36. Harris, "History, Fable and Myth," p. 25.

37. Harris, "History, Fable and Myth," pp. 13–15. See also Joyce Jonas's interpretation of vodun and the Anancy figure as cultural paradigms that suggest alternative ways of reading Caribbean fiction in her recently published book, *Anancy in the Great House* (Westport, Conn.: Greenwood Press, 1990). While Jonas formulates an approach to reading Caribbean literature based on Harris's metaphorical use of vodun and Anancy, combined with

recent anthropological and poststructuralist theories of language and perception, Patrick Taylor, in *The Narrative of Liberation* (Ithaca, N.Y., and London: Cornell University Press, 1989), analyzes the mythic structure of vodun and the creole trickster tale from the perspective of Frantz Fanon's ideas on popular culture. Emphasizing the "tragic containment" of such folk forms as the vodun ritual and the creole trickster tale, Taylor makes a distinction between "mythic narrative" and the "liberating narratives" of Caribbean writers who make a conceptual "leap" into history and consciousness. In this sense, Taylor's approach to myth and the creole folktale is similar to that of Edouard Glissant.

38. Harris, *Womb of Space*, p. 19.

2 / The Folk Imagination and History

1. González Echevarría, *The Pilgrim*, p. 107.

2. In his analysis of myth, Harry Slochower points to its capacity to function in either an adaptive or transformative role. He also observes that rebel heroes such as Dionysius and Prometheus illustrate the "revolutionary leaven" of myth by their commitment to a "tradition of freedom." See *Mythopoesis: Mythic Patterns in the Literary Classics* (Detroit, Mich.: Wayne State University Press, 1970), pp. 22–26, 34–36.

3. Carpentier, *The Kingdom of This World*, trans. Harriet de Onís (New York: Collier, 1970), p. 62. All further references, except for the Prologue (*El reino*, 1980), are from this edition.

4. For a discussion of the historical documentation of *El reino*, see Goldberg's "Estudio preliminar" in the 1980 EDHASA edition, pp. 10–15.

5. Carpentier, Prólogo, *El reino de este mundo* (1980), p. 53: "la sensación de lo maravilloso presupone una fe. Los que no creen en santos no pueden curarse con milagros de santos."

6. Chiampi, *O realismo maravilhoso*, p. 37: "Lo que se ha de entender desto de convertirse en lobos es que hay una enfermedad a que llaman los médicos manía lupina." My translation.

7. For the historical background of the Haitian Revolution see C. L. R. James's classic study *The Black Jacobins* (New York: Vintage Books, 1963), originally published in 1938.

8. C. L. R. James, *The Black Jacobins*, pp. 85–89, 91–93.

9. See Carpentier, *La música en Cuba* (Mexico: Fondo de Cultura Económica, 1979), pp. 121–35, 136–52.

10. See C. L. R. James, *The Black Jacobins*, pp. 241–88.

11. Carpentier, *Tientos y diferencias*, p. 107.

12. See Carpentier, "La cultura de los pueblos que habitan en las tierras del Caribe," *Casa* (1980), pp. 5–6. On this point, C. L. R. James and Carpentier concur. See James's analysis of the Haitian struggle for independence in *Black Jacobins*, pp. 356–77. James writes that "liberty was far more

concrete for former slaves than the elusive forms of political democracy in France" (357).

13. Chiampi notes in her discussion of Carpentier's concept of the marvelous that while he asserts the rational basis of the fantastic in *El reino*, he also indicates that it was the inability of the French colonists to relinquish "*à estreita interpretação racionalista dos fatos*" that hastened their decline in Haiti, *O realismo maravilhoso*, p. 38.

14. Carpentier repeats this symbol of cultural stasis in his reference to Canova's marble statue of Pauline Bonaparte as Venus (*El reino*, part 4, 1). Pauline's slave and masseur, Soliman, travels to Rome with Christophe's widow as the family servant. His discovery of Pauline's statue in the patio of the Borghese Palace drives him mad. Carpentier thus suggests that madness and death are the inevitable consequence of the idolatry of false gods—in this case the false values of European culture.

15. Carpentier discusses the "privileged revelation of reality" as one of the basic characteristics of the marvelous in the Prólogo, *El reino* (1980), p. 53.

16. The four novels of the "Guiana Quartet," all published by Faber and Faber of London, are: *Palace of the Peacock* (1960), *The Far Journey of Oudin* (1961), *The Whole Armour* (1962), and *The Secret Ladder* (1963).

17. See Harris, *The Whole Armour and The Secret Ladder* (London: Faber and Faber, 1973), pp. 7 and 17. All references to *The Secret Ladder* are from this edition.

18. Michael Gilkes, *Wilson Harris and the Caribbean Novel* (London: Longman, 1975), pp. 82, 97 n. 4. The shaman figure appears throughout the Quartet as the medium of the unconscious and also corresponds to Harris's concept of the role of the writer.

19. Consistent with this view of the role of the folk, the protagonist of *Palace of the Peacock* states, "We're all outside of the folk. . . . Nobody belongs yet" (p. 59).

20. Gilkes considers the members of the survey crew different aspects of Fenwick's character, who in turn represents the "psyche of Caribbean man," *Wilson Harris*, pp. 85–86, 94.

21. These two men were the shadowy figures Fenwick saw at the stelling. Gilkes interprets them as symbolic of the "dual-natured 'twin', Mercurius (Hermes), the catalytic agent in the alchemical opus," whose activity brings about the union of opposites—in this instance the resolution of Fenwick's inner conflicts (*Wilson Harris*, p. 93). Viewed as forces of intuitive understanding, the presence of the "wild twins" directs Fenwick's quest for clarity beyond the mere verification of "facts."

22. Cited by Harris from Stanley Romaine Hopper's essay "Le cri de Merlin" in the Author's Note to *The Whole Armour* and *The Secret Ladder*, p. 9.

23. Glissant, *Le quatrième siècle* (Paris: Seuil, 1964), p. 146. All further

references to this text are indicated in parentheses; translations into English are mine.

24. Glissant, *The Ripening*, trans. Michael Dash (London: Heinemann, 1985), 174–75; originally published as *La Lézarde* (Paris: Seuil, 1958).

25. Glissant, *Discours antillais*, pp. 130–31.

26. Glissant, *Discours antillais*, pp. 132, 155.

27. Glissant, *Discours antillais*, p. 428.

28. Juan Eduardo Cirlot, *A Dictionary of Symbols*, trans. Jack Sage (New York: Philosophical Library, 1971), p. 287; see also Bernadette Cailler, *Conquérants de la nuit nue* (Tübingen: Gunter Narr Verlag, 1988) on the polyvalent symbolism of the serpent in Glissant's texts, pp. 131–33. Cailler points out that the serpent is both "*sperme et venin,*" and like the *loas* of Haitian vodun may represent the benevolent as well as malevolent forces of nature (p. 132).

29. Ambivalence and ambiguity are found at all levels of Glissant's text; like Harris, he rejects the rigid polarizations of the victim/victor relationship. As Cailler observes, apparent "binary relations" in Glissant's texts are ultimately "blurred" by a marked ambiguity, so that his representations of the master/slave and maroon/planter relationships are far more subtle and complex than those usually depicted in either historical or fictional accounts of slavery, *Conquérants*, pp. 110, 114–16.

3 / The Myth of El Dorado

1. See Slochower's study of myth in modern literature, *Mythopoesis*, p. 15.

2. Slochower, *Mythopoesis*, pp. 22–23.

3. Glissant calls this longing for a primordial past *le désiré historique* in *Discours antillais*, pp. 147–50.

4. Slochower, *Mythopoesis*, pp. 22, 34. In Caribbean literature the journey is often undertaken by an intellectual or an adolescent (as can be seen in the large number of novels that deal with growing up in a colonial society); both the intellectual and the adolescent have ambiguous status in a quite literal sense.

5. More often than not the journeying protagonist in Caribbean literature (as is generally the case in other literatures also) is male. The quest of female protagonists in novels by both men and women usually takes place within the family or her own society. A notable exception is the female protagonist of Maryse Condé's *Heremakhonon* (1976), who leaves her island home for Africa.

6. Slochower, *Mythopoesis*, pp. 24–25.

7. Carpentier, *Lost Steps*, pp. 130–31. All further references to this text are cited in parentheses.

8. Wilson Harris, *Palace of the Peacock* (1960; London: Faber and Faber, 1968), p. 20. All further references to this text are cited in parentheses.

9. Chiampi, *O realismo maravilhoso*, p. 100.

10. Alberto Manguel and Gianni Guadalupi, *The Dictionary of Imaginary Places* (New York: Macmillan, 1980), pp. 108–9.

11. Since this encounter jeopardized an already precarious relationship between England and Spain, Sir Walter Raleigh's rival at the English court, the Earl of Essex, used it as an excuse to have the New World adventurer executed on charges of treason in 1617. See Naipaul's account of the Spanish and English expeditions in search of the City of Gold in *The Loss of El Dorado* (1969).

12. Ian Munro and Reinhard Sander, eds., "Interview with Wilson Harris," *Kas-Kas* (Austin: African and Afro-American Research Institute, University of Texas, 1972), p. 45.

13. Harris, "Tradition and the West Indian Novel," *Tradition, the Writer and Society* (London: New Beacon Publications, 1967), pp. 35–36.

14. See Hena Maes-Jelinek, "The Myth of El Dorado in the Caribbean Novel," *The Journal of Commonwealth Literature* 6 (June 1971): 117.

15. Kenneth Ramchand discusses the parallels between *Palace* and the history of the conquest in the Preface to *Palace*, p. 7; and in *Wilson Harris and the Modern Tradition* (Westport, Conn.: Greenwood Press, 1986), Sandra Drake relates the themes of conquest and desire in *Palace* to poststructuralist theories of language and identity, pp. 49–89.

16. Gilkes, *Wilson Harris*, p. 28.

17. Harris, "History, Fable and Myth," p. 28.

18. See Maes-Jelinek's discussion of Mariella as a "double-natured muse" within the framework of Harris's concept of the "novel of associations," *The Naked Design (A Reading of "Palace of the Peacock")* (University of Aarhus, Denmark: Dangaroo Press, 1976), pp. 21, 23.

19. See E. R. Skinner's Jungian interpretation of the journey in *Lost Steps* in *Archetypal Patterns in Four Novels of Alejo Carpentier* (Ph.D. diss., University of Kansas, 1969), pp. 113, 137.

20. The protagonist's journey is similar to the Romantics' quest for a reunion with nature as a means of achieving authenticity in art. The relationship between nature and the creative impulse is suggested throughout the initial stages of the journey, and most explicitly in the Los Altos episode where the proximity to nature first reawakens in the protagonist a strong urge to write (*Lost Steps*, p. 72). See also González Echevarría on the relationship between romanticism and the quest in *Lost Steps* in *The Pilgrim*, p. 160.

21. Though Mouche represents those modernist notions that the protagonist supposedly rejects, the symbolism of Rosario as the link to nature, the unconscious, and the creative impulse remains within the modernist poetics of the European avant-garde. See Ferdinand Alquié on the symbolism of the woman among the surrealists in *The Philosophy of Surrealism* (Ann Arbor: University of Michigan Press, 1969), pp. 84–96. Both women are projections of the protagonist's own desires and inner conflicts. Ultimately, however, Rosario doesn't live up to her role as exemplary "earth mother."

22. See Skinner, *Archetypal Patterns*, p. 114.

23. Maes-Jelinek refers to this as "moments of intensity," *The Naked Design*, p. 25.

24. See Munro and Sander, *Kas-Kas*, p. 52. Also note that in *Palace* there is a merging of consciousness among the characters of the novel, unlike the externalized forms of the inner conflict that Roberto González Echevarría recognizes in *Lost Steps* as the "unfolding of the protagonist into several selves that comment upon each other," *The Pilgrim*, pp. 165–66.

25. The protagonist of *Lost Steps* encounters a local tavern with the name "Los Recuerdos del Porvenir" (Memories of the future) in Puerto de Anunciación, the last frontier town he stops at before entering the unknown depths of the rain forest (*Lost Steps*, p. 116).

26. Maes-Jelinek, *Naked Design*, pp. 34, 35.

27. Carpentier uses a similar time frame in *Lost Steps*. The journey beyond Los Altos to the threshold of the rain forest takes seven days as does the river journey through the rain forest to El Adelantado's settlement. For a discussion of the calendar symbolism in *Lost Steps*, see González Echevarría, *The Pilgrim*, pp. 183–86.

28. In Harris's work, myth and the mythic imagination are closely related to the hermetic arts and mysticism because of their common emphasis on opposites and the transformation of ordinary reality by essentially nonrational means. See Harris on the *cauda pavonis* as a symbol of fulfillment in "History, Fable and Myth," p. 20, and Michael Gilkes on the alchemical symbolism of the seven-day journey in *Wilson Harris and the Caribbean Novel*, pp. 36–37.

29. According to Ariel Dorfman's interpretation of this episode, the protagonist of *Lost Steps* is faced with a dilemma. If he kills the leper, he knows he will destroy his notion of paradise and initiate the violence of historical reality. Yet if he does not kill the leper, he will fail to live by the laws of El Adelantado's community and must be expelled from the paradise that he is unable to defend. See *Imaginación y violencia en América* (Santiago de Chile: Editorial Universitaria, 1970), pp. 105, 106.

30. González Echevarría, *The Pilgrim*, p. 167. In this regard, González Echevarría sees the failure of the quest in *Lost Steps* as evidence of a break in the development of Carpentier's fiction, one that denies the basic premises of the 1949 prologue to *The Kingdom of This World* and subverts the metaphor of "nature as logos" (*The Pilgrim*, pp. 19, 153–54, 211). At the same time, González Echevarría maintains that this new direction in Carpentier's fiction represents a rehabilitation of the latter's surrealist past, that is, the "ludic and revolutionary spirit" of the avant-garde (*The Pilgrim*, p. 213). Yet it should be noted that language as a return to nature was also an important aspect of surrealist art. See Octavio Paz on the relationship between language and nature in surrealist poetics in "André Breton or the Quest of the Beginning," *Alternating Current*, trans. Helen R. Lane (New York: Viking, 1973), pp. 47–

59. More important, as Edouard Glissant points out in his discussion of the longing for origins, *le désiré historique*, in the literature of the Americas, the most crucial aspect of the search for origins is the process itself, *le questionnement*, the searching or quest(ion)ing. In *Los pasos* the return is impossible; it fails but, as Glissant says, its failure is meaningful (*Discours antillais*, p. 149).

31. Slochower, *Mythopoesis*, p. 25. Although *Palace of the Peacock* illustrates the ultimate power of the word to transform reality, Harris's later works reflect the problematical nature of transcendence, as we have already seen in *The Secret Ladder*, for example. In her discussion of the theme of transcendence in *Palace*, Maes-Jelinek cites Harris's novel *Heartland* (London, 1964): "The Golden Age they wished to find—The Palace of the Peacock—may never have existed for all they knew," *The Naked Design*, pp. 61, 64 n. 30.

4 / History as Mythic Discourse

1. González Echevarría, *The Pilgrim*, p. 136. See his discussion of Spengler's philosophy and its dissemination in Latin America during the 1920s, pp. 52–57; pp. 56, 161.

2. González Echevarría, *The Pilgrim*, p. 154.

3. J. Labanyi makes this point in his essay "Nature and the Historical Process in Carpentier's *El siglo de las luces*," *Bulletin of Hispanic Studies* 57 (1980): 55.

4. Labanyi, "Nature and the Historical Process," p. 55.

5. See Ariel Dorfman on this concept of myth in *El siglo de las luces* in his essay "El sentido de la historia en la obra de Alejo Carpentier," *Imaginación y violencia en América*, p. 117; and Slochower on the rebellious function of myth in *Mythopoesis*, p. 34.

6. For a brief summary of the sociohistorical background of eighteenth-century Cuba in *El siglo de las luces*, see González Echevarría, *The Pilgrim*, pp. 227–28.

7. All citations are from John Sturrock's translation, *Explosion in a Cathedral* (Boston: Little, Brown, 1963), pp. 71–72; originally published in Spanish, *El siglo de las luces* (Mexico: Compañía General de Ediciones, 1962).

8. González Echevarría uses this term in his discussion of the use of cabalistic symbolism in *El siglo* (*The Pilgrim*, pp. 237–44), which I will discuss in my comparison of a similar strategy in Harris's *Tumatumari*.

9. This episode coincides with the account of the emigration of the creole planters in the wake of the Bouckman revolt (1791) in *El reino de este mundo*.

10. Ogé's brother Vincent is based on a historical figure in the Haitian Revolution who was tortured and killed for leading an insurrection against the intransigent French colonists who refused to abide by a decree of the National Assembly that gave educated blacks and mulattoes the right to hold public office. See C. L. R. James, *The Black Jacobins*, pp. 68, 73–74, 76.

11. Dorfman, *Imaginación*, p. 119: "La Historia no es ni la línea recta del

progreso absoluto ni el círculo monótono de lo que retorna siempre igual, sino la unión de ambas categorías, reiteración y progreso, movimiento e inmovilidad, Arquetipo y tiempo: es el Espiral, repetición que cambia."

12. See González Echevarría, *The Pilgrim*, p. 247.

13. González Echevarría notes that "the transition from 1799 to 1800 marks the chronological center of the action (1789-1809)" as opposed to the "textual center" of the novel in subchapter 24 where the *caracol* appears as symbol of the movement of history. He considers the displaced textual and chronological centers of *El siglo* another example of Carpentier's use of the spiral: "This displacement of centers is analogous to the spiral's. The centers do not constitute a fixed chronological or textual fulcrum, but instead provide, as does the spiral, a movable, phantasmatic axis, constantly doing and undoing itself, around which the action of the novel revolves: a 'law of convolutions', not of mirror images, presides over the structure of the novel" (*Pilgrim*, pp. 249, 250).

14. Cited from Charles Poncé, *Kaballah: An Introduction for the World Today* (1973) by González Echevarría in *The Pilgrim*, pp. 240-41. The cabala symbolism in *El siglo* is suggested by the epigraph to the novel (*Las palabras no caen en el vacío*, Words are not in vain), which is taken from the *Zohar* or *Book of Splendor*, a mystical commentary on the Hebrew Scriptures that was written in thirteenth-century Spain.

15. See Dorfman on this point in *Imaginación*, p. 108.

16. Erich Neumann, *The Great Mother: An Analysis of the Archetype*, (New York: Pantheon Books, 1955), pp. 325-26, 331.

17. Neumann, *The Great Mother*, p. 331.

18. Esteban had always associated Sofia's name with the Byzantine dome, "wrapped in palms from the Tree of Life and surrounded by Archons in all the mystery of Intact Womanhood," *Explosion in a Cathedral*, p. 254.

19. The events that take place after Sofia's departure from French Guiana are reconstructed by her brother Carlos in the final chapter of the novel. Although Carlos only plays a minor role in the development of the narrative, he serves as an important link between the historical events that take place in Spain and those that will take place in the New World in the aftermath of the Napoleonic invasion. González Echevarría draws a parallel between Carlos and the historical figure Carlos Manuel de Céspedes who led the Cuban revolt against the Spanish in 1868 (*The Pilgrim*, pp. 231, 232).

20. See Gilkes, *Wilson Harris*, p. 122 on memory in *Tumatumari*.

21. Munro and Sander, *Kas-Kas*, p. 52.

22. Wilson Harris, *Fossil and Psyche* (Occasional Publication, African and Afro-American Studies Research Center, University of Texas at Austin, 1974), pp. 2-3.

23. Wilson Harris, *Ascent to Omai* (London: Faber and Faber, 1970), p. 9, 51.

24. Michael Gilkes, *The West Indian Novel* (Boston: Twayne Publishers,

1981), p. 146. See also Frances A. Yates on the relationship between prudence and memory; she cites Cicero's definition of the cardinal virtue of Prudence as "memory, intelligence and foresight" in the *The Art of Memory* (Chicago: University of Chicago Press, 1966), pp. 20–21.

25. Hena Maes-Jelinek, "Wilson Harris," *West Indian Literature*, ed. Bruce King, p. 190. Compare Joyce Adler's critique of the role of Prudence in "Wilson Harris's *Tumatumari* and the Family of Man," *Critics on Caribbean Literature*, ed. Edward Baugh, pp. 113–20. Sandra Drake, on the other hand, maintains that Prudence "succeeds in her own right" since she accomplishes what the male characters of *Tumatumari* fail to do, the task of (re)conceiving history, *Wilson Harris* (1986), pp. 94–95.

26. Munro and Sander, *Kas-Kas*, pp. 51, 52.

27. Wilson Harris, *Tumatumari* (London: Faber and Faber, 1968), p. 23; all further references to this text are cited in parentheses.

28. Similar to the cabalistic symbolism of the triad in *El siglo*, the alchemical process is the basis of Harris's metaphorical use of the triad in *Tumatumari*. See Gilkes, *Wilson Harris*, p. 129, on the alchemical symbolism in Harris's novel.

29. Neumann, *The Great Mother*, pp. 57, 319; he also points out that the transformation of the masculine is often manifested as a "surprise attack," such as lightning (p. 55), which is similar to Roi's "electrification" in the concrete pit.

30. Cirlot, *Dictionary of Symbols*, p. 320.

31. For background information on this period in Guyanese politics, see Gordon K. Lewis, "Emergence of National Society," *The Growth of the Modern West Indies* (New York: Monthly Review Press 1968), pp. 259–88.

32. The same year that Hugh was born, 1938, Tenby wrote an essay on the "Population Question" in which he quotes extensively from the creole historian A. R. F. Webber on the failure of immigration policies (both forced and voluntary) in Guyana (*Tumatumari*, pp. 97–99). In *The Growth of the Modern West Indies*, Gordon K. Lewis points to the colonial population policy as one of the major causes of racial polarization in contemporary Guyanese politics (pp. 259–60). Henry Tenby's children—Prudence, Hugh, and Pamela—therefore represent the unintegrated cultures of America, Africa, and Europe in Guyana, a principal source of conflict in the struggle for independence between 1953 and 1966.

33. According to Neumann, the Gorgon is associated with the underworld and death. She is therefore a symbol of eclipse, the night sun. The serpents writhing around her head are a form of "negative radiation," but she is not an entirely negative force since she also gives birth to the day sun (*The Great Mother*, pp. 22–23, 166).

34. Glissant, *La case du commandeur* (Paris: Seuil, 1981). All citations of passages from this text are my translations.

35. See Glissant's discussion of "history as psychoneurosis" in *Discours*

antillais, pp. 133–34, which is related to Frantz Fanon's analysis of the psychopathology of racism and colonialism in *Black Skin, White Masks* (1967).

36. Glissant, *Discours antillais*, p. 153. In his discussion of the difference between the Caribbean folktale and traditional myth, Glissant maintains, "Le Conte nous a donné le Nous, en exprimant de manière implicite que nous avons à le conquérir," The Tale has given us the We, by expressing in an implicit way that we must conquer it, *Discours antillais*, p. 152. See also *L'Intention poétique*, pp. 187, 191 on collective memory as "our lack and our most urgent need."

37. Traditionally throughout the Caribbean, the conch shell was used among the slaves to communicate messages, to call workers to the canefields, to sound out calls of rebellion, or to announce some calamity, such as death. In Carpentier's *El reino* and *El siglo*, the conch shell is associated with rebellion and historical change. Notably, because of its womblike configuration, the conch shell is also symbolic of the feminine, particularly female rebellion as in Michelle Cliff's novel *Abeng* (Trumansburg, N.Y.: The Crossing Press, 1984).

38. Cinna Chimène welcomes her daughter as the "Mary of Black Women (Negresses)." The Longoué and Celat women in Glissant's novels recall the proud peasant women of Guadeloupe in Simone Schwarz-Bart's *Pluie et vent sur Télumée Miracle* (Paris: Seuil, 1972). The women in Glissant's texts, as Bernadette Cailler points out, are "never fooled by grand ideas" and serve as a "bridge" between men obsessed with heroic aspirations and "ordinary folk." See "Edouard Glissant: A Creative Critic," *World Literature Today* 63. 4 (Autumn 1989): 591.

39. The object of Pythagore's search is Béhanzin, the King of Dahomey, who fought against French penetration of Africa and was deported to Martinique. In *Discours antillais*, Glissant refers to this barely acknowledged historical event as a "curiosity," which he believes (like the *bête-longue*) still lurks in the Martinican unconscious, p. 496.

40. See Glissant's discussion of orality and writing in *Discours antillais*, pp. 237–42. Compare Isidore Okpewho, "Elements of Oral Narrative Style," *The Epic in Africa: Toward a Poetics of the Oral Performance* (New York: Columbia University Press, 1979) and Walter J. Ong, *Orality and Literacy* (London: Methuen, 1982); as well as Edward Kamau Brathwaite's study of orality in Anglophone Caribbean literature and popular culture, *History of the Voice* (London: New Beacon Books, 1984).

5 / The Poetics of Identity and Difference

1. Wilson Harris, *Black Marsden (a tabula rasa comedy)* (London: Faber and Faber, 1972), pp. 9–10; all further references are cited in parentheses. In a later novel, *Carnival* (London: Faber and Faber, 1985), the concepts of

duality and ambivalence associated with the Caledonian antisyzygy in *Black Marsden* are identified with the ludic elements of the Caribbean folk festival. Harris uses the carnival metaphor as a means of revising and reenvisioning notions of identity, power, and creativity. See Maes-Jelinek, " 'Carnival' and Creativity in Wilson Harris's Fiction," *The Literate Imagination: Essays on the Novels of Wilson Harris,* ed. Gilkes (London: Macmillan, 1989), pp. 45–61.

2. From a Jungian perspective, Michael Gilkes interprets Marsden as "both the hero's personal (and archetypal) shadow and the creative magus-like activity of the author himself," *Wilson Harris,* p. 146.

3. See Gilkes, *Wilson Harris,* p. 149.

4. Maes-Jelinek, *Wilson Harris,* p. 142.

5. Knife appears in many guises; he is beggar and assassin, and although he is Marsden's "white purgatorial Knife," he resembles a Black Knife that Goodrich once met in Jamaica. Because of his various racial identities, Maes-Jelinek refers to him as the "face of the collectivity," associated with racial and political polarizations (*Wilson Harris,* p. 142). Similarly, Gilkes sees him as a symbol of the "double-edged nature of violence in which victim and victor are *both* affected" (*Wilson Harris,* p. 147). He may also be interpreted in a more general sense as Harris's representation of the harsh ambiguities of life.

6. In the journey through Namless, Marsden is identified with the Director-General; earlier in the novel Knife is referred to as a "rude parody of Marsden's head of state" (*Black Marsden,* p. 57).

7. *Concierto barroco,* trans. Asa Zatz (Tulsa, Oklahoma: Council Oak Books and University of Tulsa, 1988), p. 7. All citations are from this edition of the novel, which was originally published in Spanish (Mexico: Siglo Veintiuno, 1974).

8. Specific dates are not mentioned in the novel, but are verifiable by references to certain cultural events, such as the first performances of famous operas and concerts. See González Echevarría on the calculation of historical dates in *Concierto* (*The Pilgrim,* pp. 266–68).

9. The term *indiano* in Spanish refers to a person from the Indies. It may be used for a Spanish American or a West Indian, but historically the term refers to a person returning to Europe from South America with great wealth.

10. Pedro Barreda, *The Black Protagonist in the Cuban Novel* (Amherst: University of Massachusetts Press, 1979), p. 14. Although Barreda dismisses Balboa's portrayal of the epic hero Salvador as just another European stereotype of the black man, akin to the notion of the noble savage, the Bayamese slave in *Espejo de la paciencia* presents a powerful image that is almost totally lacking in subsequent treatments of black characters in Cuban literature until the poetry of Nicolás Guillén and the novels of Antonio Zambrana and Alejo Carpentier.

11. See González Echevarría on intertextuality in this novel (*The Pilgrim,* pp. 267–68).

12. Pedro Barreda's criticism of Balboa's poem in *The Black Protagonist in the Cuban Novel* is a good example of this attitude.

13. See González Echevarría on the calculation of this date; he also notes that 26 December is Carpentier's birthday (*The Pilgrim*, p. 268).

14. González Echevarría describes the carnival revelry at the conservatory as the "whirlwindlike center" in which the occult traditions of Afro-Cuban religious practices and the cabala are intermingled (*The Pilgrim*, p. 266).

15. The Mexican's experience may be interpreted as a semiautobiographical reference to Carpentier's own experience in Europe in the 1930s and his response to the surrealist interest in the legends and myths of the Americas.

16. Giambattista Vico, *The New Science* (Ithaca, N.Y.: Cornell University Press, 1968), pp. 73, 119–20, 128.

17. In this regard, Filomeno's expatriate experience corresponds to that of many black musicians who went to Europe in the 1920s and 1930s (and continue to do so) to escape racial prejudice at home.

18. González Echevarría points this out in *The Pilgrim*, p. 270, and cites Cirlot on the symbolism of the double figure eight as a sign of regeneration.

Selected Bibliography

Alexis, Jacques Stéphen. *Les Arbes musiciens*. Paris: Gallimard, 1957.

———. *Compère Général Soleil*. Paris: Gallimard, 1955.

———. "Du réalisme merveilleux des Haïtiens." *Présence Africaine* 8–10 (June–November 1956): 245–71.

Alquié, Ferdinand. *The Philosophy of Surrealism*. Trans. Bernard Waldrop. Ann Arbor: University of Michigan Press, 1969.

Bader, Wolfgang. "Poétique antillaise, poétique de la relation—Interview avec Edouard Glissant." *Komparatistische Hefte* (University of Bayreuth) 9/10 (1984): 83–100.

Balakian, Anna. *The Literary Origins of Surrealism*. New York: New York University Press, 1965.

Barreda, Pedro. *The Black Protagonist in the Cuban Novel*. Amherst: University of Massachusetts Press, 1979.

Barthes, Roland. *Mythologies*. Trans. Annette Lavers. New York and London: Jonathan Cape, 1972.

Baugh, Edward, ed. *Critics on Caribbean Literature*. New York: St. Martin's Press, 1978.

Brathwaite, Edward (Kamau). *The Arrivants: A New World Trilogy*. London: Oxford University Press, 1973.

———. *Contradictory Omens: Cultural Diversity and Integration in the Caribbean.* 1974. Kingston: Savacou, 1985.

———. *Folk Culture of the Slaves in Jamaica.* Rev. ed. London: New Beacon Books, 1981.

———. *History of the Voice: The Development of Nation Language in Anglophone Caribbean poetry.* London: New Beacon Books, 1984.

———. "Presencia africana en la literatura del Caribe." Moreno Fraginals, *Africa en América Latina* 52–184.

Breton, André. *Manifestes du surréalisme.* 1962. Paris: Gallimard, 1972.

Cailler, Bernadette. *Conquérants de la nuit nue: Edouard Glissant et l'H(h)istoire antillaise.* Tübingen: Gunter Narr Verlag, 1988.

———. "Edouard Glissant: A Creative Critic." *World Literature Today* 63.4 (Autumn 1989): 589–92.

CARÉ (Centre Antillais de Recherches et d'Etudes). "Edouard Glissant." Special Issue 10 (avril 1983). Paris: Editions Caribéennes.

Carpentier, Alejo. *El arpa y la sombra.* Mexico: Siglo Veintiuno, 1980.

———. "Autobiografía de urgencia." *Insula* 218 (1965): 3, 13.

———. *Concierto barroco.* Mexico: Siglo Veintiuno, 1974; La Habana: Editorial Arte y Literatura del Instituto Cubano del Libro, 1975. Trans. Asa Zatz, *Concierto Barroco.* Tulsa, Oklahoma: Council Oak Books and University of Tulsa, 1988.

———. *Cuentos completos.* Barcelona: Bruguera, 1980.

———. "La cultura de los pueblos que habitan en las tierras del Mar Caribe." *Casa de las Americas* 20 (1980): 2–8.

———. *Ecue-Yamba-O. Novela Afrocubana.* 1933. Buenos Aires: Editorial Xanadu, 1968.

———. *Guerra del tiempo.* 1958. Mexico: Compañía General de Ediciones, 1962.

———. *La música en Cuba.* 1946. Mexico: Fondo de Cultura Económica, 1979.

———. *La novela latinoamericana en vísperas de un nuevo siglo y otros ensayos.* Mexico: Siglo Veintiuno, 1981.

———. *Los pasos perdidos.* Mexico: EDIAPSA, 1953. Trans. Harriet de Onís, *The Lost Steps.* New York: Avon Books, 1979.

———. "Prólogo." *El reino de este mundo.* 1949. "Estudio preliminar" by Florinda Friedmann de Goldberg. Barcelona: EDHASA, 1980. Trans. Harriet de Onís, *The Kingdom of this World.* New York: Collier, 1970. [The prologue is not included in the English translation.]

———. *El recurso del método.* Mexico: Siglo Veintiuno, 1974. Trans. Frances Partridge, *Reasons of State.* New York: Alfred A. Knopf, 1976.

———. *El siglo de las luces.* Mexico: Campañía General de Ediciones, 1962. Trans. John Sturrock, *Explosion in a Cathedral.* Boston: Little, Brown, 1963.

———. *Tientos y diferencias.* 1964. Montevideo: Editorial Arca, 1967.

Casa de las Américas. "Del simposio sobre la identidad cultural caribeña." Carifesta Issue 118 (1980).

Case, F. I. *The Crisis of Identity: Studies in the Guadeloupean and Martiniquan Novel.* Sherbrooke, Québec: Naaman, 1985.

———. "The Novels of Edouard Glissant." *Black Images* 2 (1973): 3–12.

Césaire, Aimé. *Cahier d'un retour au pays natal.* 1939. Paris: Présence Africaine, 1956.

———. *Discours sur le colonialisme.* Paris: Présence Africaine, 1955.

———. *La tragédie du roi Christophe.* Paris: Présence Africaine, 1963.

Chiampi, Irlemar. *O realismo maravilhoso: forma e ideologia no romance hispano-americano.* São Paulo: Editora Perspectiva, 1980.

———. "La reescritura de Carpentier, según Roberto González Echevarría." *Revista Iberoamericana* 102–103 (1978): 157–64.

Cirlot, Juan Eduardo. *A Dictionary of Symbols.* Trans. Jack Sage. 2d ed. New York: Philosophical Library, 1971.

Cliff, Michelle. *Abeng.* Trumansburg, N.Y.: The Crossing Press, 1984.

Coulthard, G. R. "El mito indígena en la literatura hispanoamericana contemporánea." *Cuadernos Americanos* 156 (1968): 164–73.

———. *Race and Colour in Caribbean Literature.* London: Oxford University Press, 1962.

Crahan, Margaret E., and Franklin W. Knight, eds. *Africa and the Caribbean: The Legacies of a Link.* Baltimore: Johns Hopkins University Press, 1979.

Cudjoe, Selwyn Reginald. *Resistance and Caribbean Literature.* Chicago and Athens, Ohio: Ohio University Press, 1980.

———. "The Role of Resistance in the Caribbean Novel." Ph.D. diss., Cornell University, 1976.

Culler, Jonathan. *Structuralist Poetics.* Ithaca, N.Y.: Cornell University Press, 1975.

Dash, Michael. "Ariel's Discourse: French Caribbean Writing After the Storm." *Journal of West Indian Literature* 1 (1986): 49–58.

———. Introduction. Glissant, *Caribbean Discourse* xi–xlvii.

———. "Jacques Stéphen Alexis." Monograph. *Black Images* 3 (1975): 6–62.

———. *Literature and Ideology in Haiti, 1915–1961.* Totowa, N.J.: Barnes and Noble, 1981.

———. "Marvelous Realism—The Way Out of Negritude." *Black Images* 3.1 (January 1974): 80–95.

———. "Writing the Body: Edouard Glissant's Poetics of Re-membering." *World Literature Today* 63.4 (1989): 609–12.

Dawes, Neville. *Prolegomena to Caribbean Literature.* Kingston: Institute of Jamaica, 1977.

Depestre, René. *Un arc-en-ciel pour l'Occident chrétien, poème mystère vaudou.* Paris: Présence Africaine, 1966.

————. *Bonjour et adieu à la négritude*. Paris: Robert Laffont, 1980.

————. *Le mât de cocagne*. Paris: Gallimard, 1979.

Dorfman, Ariel. "El sentido de la historia en la obra de Alejo Carpentier." *Imaginación y violencia en América*. Santiago de Chile: Editorial Universitaria, 1970. 93–137.

Drake, Sandra. *Wilson Harris and the Modern Tradition: A New Architecture of the World*. Westport, Conn.: Greenwood Press, 1986.

Durán Luzio, Juan. *La lectura histórica de la novela*. Costa Rica: Editorial de la Universidad Nacional, 1982.

Eliade, Mircea. *Birth and Rebirth: The Religious Meanings of Initiation in Human Culture*. Trans. Willard Trask. New York: Harper, 1958.

————. *The Myth of the Eternal Return*. Trans. Willard Trask. New York: Pantheon Books, 1954.

Fanon, Frantz. *Les damnés de la terre*. Paris: F. Maspero, 1961. Trans. Constance Farrington, *The Wretched of the Earth*. New York: Grove Press, 1968.

————. *Peau noire, masques blancs*. Paris: Seuil, 1952. Trans. Charles Lam Markmann, *Black Skin, White Masks*. New York: Grove Press, 1967.

Fell, Claudio. "Encuentro con Alejo Carpentier." *Estudios de literatura hispanoamericana contemporánea*. Mexico: Secretaria de Educación Pública, 1976. 7–17.

Fernández Retamar, R. *Caliban and Other Essays*. Trans. Edward Baker. Foreword by Frederic Jameson. Minneapolis: University of Minnesota Press, 1989.

————. *Calibán: apuntes sobre la cultura de nuestra América*. Buenos Aires: Editorial La Pleyade, 1973.

————. "Our America and the West." *Social Text* 15 (Fall 1986): 1–25.

Fowler, Carolyn. *A Knot in the Thread: The Life and Works of Jacques Roumain*. Washington, D.C.: Howard University Press, 1980.

Franco, Jean. *Historia de la literatura hispanoamericana*. Barcelona: Editorial Ariel, 1985.

————. *An Introduction to Spanish American Literature*. London: Cambridge University Press, 1969.

Frye, Northrop, et al. *Myth and Symbol: Critical Approaches and Applications*. Lincoln: University of Nebraska Press, 1963.

Fuentes, Carlos. *La nueva novela hispanoamericana*. Mexico: Editorial Joaquin Mortiz, 1969.

Gershman, Herbert S. *The Surrealist Revolution in France*. Ann Arbor: University of Michigan Press, 1974.

Giacoman, Helmy F., ed. *Homenaje a Alejo Carpentier*. New York: Las Americas, 1970.

Gilkes, Michael. *The West Indian Novel*. Boston: Twayne Publishers, 1981.

————. *Wilson Harris and the Caribbean Novel*. London: Longman, 1975.

————, ed. *The Literate Imagination: Essays on the Novels of Wilson Harris*. London: Macmillan, 1989.

Glissant, Edouard. "Beyond Babel." *World Literature Today* 63.4 (1989): 561–63.

————. *Caribbean Discourse: Selected Essays*. Trans. and intro. Michael Dash. Charlottesville: University Press of Virginia, 1989.

————. *La case du commandeur*. Paris: Seuil, 1981.

————. *Le discours antillais*. Paris: Seuil, 1981.

————. *L'intention poétique*. Paris: Seuil, 1969.

————. *La Lézarde*. Paris: Seuil, 1958. Trans. and intro. Michael Dash, *The Ripening*. London: Heinemann, 1985.

————. *Mahagony*. Paris: Seuil, 1987.

————. *Malemort*. Paris: Seuil, 1975.

————. *Monsieur Toussaint*. Paris: Seuil, 1961. Trans. Joseph G. Foster and Barbara A. Franklin, intro. and notes Juris Silenieks, *Monsieur Toussaint*. Washington, D.C.: Three Continents Press, 1981.

————. *Pays rêvé, pays réel: poème*. Paris: Seuil, 1985.

————. *Poèmes*. Paris: Seuil, 1965.

————. *Poétique de la Relation*. Paris: Gallimard, 1990.

————. *Le quatrième siècle*. Paris: Seuil, 1964.

González Echevarría, Roberto. *Alejo Carpentier: The Pilgrim at Home*. Ithaca, N.Y.: Cornell University Press, 1977.

————, ed. "Hispanic Caribbean Literature." Special Issue. *Latin American Literary Review* 16 (1980).

————. "Isla a su vuelo fugitiva: Carpentier y el realismo mágico." *Revista Iberoamericana* 40 (1974): 9–62.

————. *The Voices of the Masters: Writing and Authority in Modern Latin American Literature*. Austin: University of Texas Press, 1985.

Gould, Eric. *Mythical Intentions in Modern Literature*. Princeton, N.J.: Princeton University Press, 1981.

Harris, Leonie B. "Myths in West Indian Consciousness: An Examination of George Lamming's *Natives of My Person*." *Critical Issues in West Indian Literature: Selected Papers from West Indian Literature Conferences, 1981–1983*. Ed. Erika Sollish Smilotz and Roberta Quarles Knowles. Parkersburg, Ind.: Caribbean Books, 1984.

Harris, Wilson. *The Age of the Rainmakers*. London: Faber and Faber, 1971.

————. *Ascent to Omai*. London: Faber and Faber, 1970.

————. *Black Marsden (a tabula rasa comedy)*. London: Faber and Faber, 1972.

————. *Carnival*. London: Faber and Faber, 1985.

————. *Companions of the Day and Night*. London: Faber and Faber, 1975.

————. *Eternity to Season*. Guyana: 1954. Reprint. London and Port of Spain: New Beacon Books, 1978.

————. *Explorations: A Selection of Talks and Articles, 1966/1988.* Ed. and intro. Hena Maes-Jelinek. Mundelstrup, Denmark: Dangaroo Press, 1981.

————. *The Far Journey of Oudin.* London: Faber and Faber, 1961.

————. *Fossil and Psyche.* Occasional Publication. African and Afro-American Studies and Research Center. Austin: University of Texas, 1974.

————. *Four Banks of the River Space.* London: Faber and Faber, 1990.

————. *Genesis of the Clowns.* London: Faber and Faber, 1977.

————. *Heartland.* London: Faber and Faber, 1964.

————. "History, Fable and Myth in the Caribbean and Guianas." *Caribbean Quarterly* 16 (June 1970): 1–32.

————. *The Infinite Rehearsal.* London: Faber and Faber, 1987.

————. "Interior of the Novel: Amerindian/European/African Relations." *National Identity.* Ed. K. L. Goodwin. London: Heinemann Educational Books, 1970.

————. "Literacy and the Imagination." Gilkes, *The Literate Imagination* 13–30.

————. "The Native Phenomenon." *Common Wealth.* Ed. Anna Rutherford. Aarhus, Denmark: University of Aarhus, 1971.

————. *Palace of the Peacock.* 1960. London: Faber and Faber, 1968.

————. "The Phenomenal Legacy." *Literary Half-Yearly* 11 (1970): 1–6.

————. *The Secret Ladder.* London: Faber and Faber, 1963.

————. *The Sleepers of Roraima.* London: Faber and Faber, 1970.

————. *Tradition, the Writer and Society.* London: New Beacon Publications, 1967.

————. *The Tree of the Sun.* London: Faber and Faber, 1978.

————. *Tumatumari.* London: Faber and Faber, 1968.

————. "The Unresolved Constitution." *Caribbean Quarterly* 14 (1968): 43–47.

————. *The Whole Armour.* London: Faber and Faber, 1962.

————. *The Whole Armour and The Secret Ladder.* London: Faber and Faber, 1973.

————. *The Womb of Space.* Westport, Conn.: Greenwood Press, 1983.

Hearne, John. "The Fugitive in the Forest: Four Novels by Wilson Harris." *Modern Black Novelists.* Ed. M. G. Cooke. Englewood Cliffs, N.J.: Prentice-Hall, 1971. 177–87.

Hermand, Jost, and Evelyn Torton Beck. "Concerning the Dialectics of Culture." *Interpretive Synthesis.* New York: Frederick Ungar, 1975. 183–206.

Horowitz, Michael M., ed. *Peoples and Cultures of the Caribbean.* Garden City, N.Y.: The Natural History Press, Doubleday, 1971.

Howard, W. J. "Wilson Harris's *Guiana Quartet:* From Personal Myth to National Identity." *Readings in Commonwealth Literature.* Ed. William Walsh. London: Oxford University Press, 1973. 314–28.

Irish, J. A. George. "Magical Realism: A Search for Caribbean and Latin American Roots." *Revista/Review Interamericana* 4 (Fall 1974): 411–21.

James, C. L. R. *The Black Jacobins: Toussaint L'Ouverture and the San Domingo Revolution*. 2d. ed., rev. New York: Vintage Books, 1963.

James, Louis. *The Islands in Between*. London: Oxford University Press, 1968.

Jonas, Joyce. *Anancy in the Great House: Ways of Reading West Indian Fiction*. Westport, Conn.: Greenwood Press, 1990.

Jung, Carl G. *Man and His Symbols*. New York: Doubleday, 1964.

——. *Psychology and Alchemy*. Trans. R. F. C. Hull. 2d. ed., rev. Princeton, N.J.: Princeton University Press, 1968.

——. *Symbols of Transformation*. Trans. R. F. C. Hull. 2d. ed., rev. Princeton, N.J.: Princeton University Press, 1967.

Kesteloot, Lilyan. *Les écrivains noirs de langue française: naissance d'une littérature*. Brussels: Institut de Sociologie de l'Université Libre, 1963.

King, Bruce, ed. *West Indian Literature*. Hamden, Conn.: Archon Books, 1979.

Kirk, G. S. *Myth: Its Meaning and Function in Ancient and Other Cultures*. London: Cambridge University Press; Berkeley: University of California Press, 1970.

Knight, Franklin W. *The Caribbean: The Genesis of a Fragmented Nationalism*. New York: Oxford University Press, 1978.

Knight, Franklin W., and Colin A. Palmer, eds. *The Modern Caribbean*. Chapel Hill: University of North Carolina Press, 1989.

Knight, Vere W. "Edouard Glissant: The Novel as History Rewritten." *Black Images* 3 (1974): 19–33.

Labanyi, J. "Nature and the Historical Process in Carpentier's *El siglo de las luces*." *Bulletin of Hispanic Studies* 57 (1980): 55–66.

Labastida, Jaime. "Alejo Carpentier: realidad y conocimiento estético (sobre *El recurso del método*)." *Casa de las Américas* 87 (1975): 21–31.

Lamming, George. *In the Castle of My Skin*. New York: McGraw Hill, 1953.

——. *Natives of My Person*. New York: Holt, Rinehart and Winston, 1972.

——. *The Pleasures of Exile*. 1960. London: Allison & Busby, 1984.

——. "The Role of the Intellectual in the Caribbean." *Cimarrón* 1 (1985): 13–22.

——. *Season of Adventure*. 1960. London: Allison & Busby, 1979.

——. *Water with Berries*. London: Longman, 1971.

Lévi-Strauss, Claude. "History and Dialectic." *The Savage Mind*. Chicago: University of Chicago Press, 1966. 245–69.

——. "The Science of the Concrete." *The Savage Mind* 1–33.

——. "The Structural Study of Myth." 1955. Sebeok, *Myth: A Symposium* 81–106.

Lewis, Gordon K. *The Growth of the Modern West Indies*. New York: Monthly Review Press, 1968.

———. *Main Currents in Caribbean Thought: The Historical Evolution of Caribbean Society in Its Ideological Aspects, 1492–1900*. Baltimore: Johns Hopkins University Press, 1983.

———. "Some Reflections on the Leading Intellectual Currents That Have Shaped the Caribbean Experience: 1950–1984." *Cimarrón* 1 (1985): 23–40.

Leyburn, James G. *The Haitian People*. New Haven, Conn.: Yale University Press, 1966.

Loveluck, Juan. "*Los pasos perdidos:* Jason y el nuevo vellocino." *Atenea* 40 (1963): 120–34.

Lucente, Gregory L. "The Creation of Myth's Rhetoric: Views of the Mythic Sign." *Comparative Literature Studies* 18 (1981): 50–68.

———. *The Narrative of Realism and Myth*. Baltimore: Johns Hopkins University Press, 1979.

Luis, William, ed. *Voices from Under: Black Narrative in Latin America and the Caribbean*. Westport, Conn.: Greenwood Press, 1984.

Maes-Jelinek, Hena. "'Carnival' and Creativity in Wilson Harris's Fiction." Gilkes, *The Literate Imagination* 45–61.

———. "The Myth of El Dorado in the Caribbean Novel." *Journal of Commonwealth Literature* 6 (June 1971): 113–28.

———. *The Naked Design: A Reading of "Palace of the Peacock."* University of Aarhus, Denmark: Dangaroo Press, 1976.

———. "Natural and Psychological Landscapes." *Journal of Commonwealth Literature* 7 (1972): 117–20.

———. *Wilson Harris*. Boston: Twayne Publishers, 1982.

———. "Wilson Harris." King, *West Indian Literature* 179–95.

Manguel, Alberto, and Gianni Guadalupi. *The Dictionary of Imaginary Places*. New York: Macmillan, 1980.

Mannheim, Karl. *Ideology and Utopia*. Trans. Louis Wirth and Edward Shils. New York: Harcourt, Brace and World, 1936.

Márquez, Roberto. "Nationalism, Nation, and Ideology." Knight and Palmer, *The Modern Caribbean* 293–340.

Márquez Rodríguez, Alexis. *Lo barroco y lo real-maravilloso en la obra de Alejo Carpentier*. 2d. ed. Mexico: Siglo XXI, 1984.

———. *La obra narrativa de Alejo Carpentier*. Buenos Aires: Fernando Garcia Cambeiro, 1972.

Mazziotti, Nora, ed. *Historia y mito en la obra de Alejo Carpentier*. Buenos Aires: Fernando Garcia Cambeiro, 1972.

Méndez, José Luis. "Literature and National Liberation in the Caribbean." *Caliban* 1 (1975): 5–20.

Métraux, Alfred. *Voodoo in Haiti*. Trans. Hugo Charteris, intro. Sidney W. Mintz. New York: Schocken Books, 1972.

Mintz, Sidney W., and Sally Price, eds. *Caribbean Contours*. Baltimore: Johns Hopkins University Press, 1985.

Moore, Gerald. *The Chosen Tongue*. New York: Harper and Row, 1970.

Moreno Fraginals, Manuel, ed. *Africa en América Latina*. Mexico: Siglo Veintiuno, 1977.

Müller-Bergh, Klaus. *Alejo Carpentier: estudio biográfico-crítico*. Long Island City, N.Y.: Las Americas Publishing, 1972.

———, ed. *Asedios a Alejo Carpentier*. Santiago de Chile: Editorial Universitaria, 1972.

———. "The Persistence of the Marvelous." *Review* 28 (1981): 25–26.

Munro, Ian, and Reinhard Sander, eds. "Interview with Wilson Harris." *Kas-Kas*. Austin: African and Afro-American Research Institute, University of Texas, 1972. 43–56.

Nadal, Mayra. "El mito de Africa en la novela antillana de expresión francesa (Martinica y Guadalupe)." *Caribe* 4–5 (1983–1984): 41–57.

Naipaul, V. S. *The Loss of El Dorado*. 1969. New York: Penguin, 1973.

———. *The Middle Passage*. New York: Macmillan, 1962.

Nettleford, Rex. *Caribbean Cultural Identity*. Los Angeles: Center for Afro-American Studies and UCLA Latin American Center Publications, University of California, 1978.

Neumann, Erich. *Art and the Creative Unconscious*. Trans. Ralph Manheim. New York: Pantheon Books, 1959.

———. *The Great Mother: An Analysis of the Archetype*. Trans. Ralph Manheim. New York: Pantheon Books, 1955.

———. *The Origins and History of Consciousness*. Trans. R. F. C. Hull. New York: Pantheon Books, 1954.

Okpewho, Isidore. *The Epic in Africa: Towards a Poetics of the Oral Performance*. New York: Columbia University Press, 1979.

———. "Rethinking Myth." *African Literature Today* 11 (1980): 5–23.

Ong, Walter J. *Orality and Literacy: The Technologizing of the Word*. London: Methuen, 1982.

Ormerod, Beverley. "Beyond Negritude: Some Aspects of the Work of Edouard Glissant." *Contemporary Literature* 15 (1974): 360–69.

———. "Discourse and Dispossession: Edouard Glissant's Image of Contemporary Martinique." *Caribbean Quarterly* 27.4 (1981): 1–12.

———. "French Caribbean Literature: The Contemporary Situation." *Literary Half-Yearly* West Indian Number 11 (1970): 113–26.

———. *An Introduction to the French Caribbean Novel*. London: Heinemann, 1985.

Ortega, Julio. *The Poetics of Change: The Spanish-American Narrative*. Trans. Galen D. Greaser with the author. Austin: University of Texas Press, 1984.

Pageaux, Daniel-Henri. *Images et mythes d'Haïti*. Paris: Harmattan, 1984.

————. "*El Reino de este mundo* ou les chemins de l'utopie." *Komparatistische Hefte* 9/10 (1984): 57–67.

Paz, Octavio. *Alternating Current*. Trans. Helen R. Lane. New York: Viking, 1973.

————. *El arco y la lira*. Mexico: Fondo de Cultura Económica, 1956.

————. *Conjunctions and Disjunctions*. Trans. Helen R. Lane. New York: Viking Press, 1974.

Présence Africaine. "Présence antillaise: Guadeloupe-Guyane-Martinique." Special Number 121–122 (1982).

Price, Richard, ed. *Maroon Societies: Rebel Slave Communities in the Americas*. 2d ed. Baltimore: Johns Hopkins University Press, 1979.

Ramchand, Kenneth. *The West Indian Novel and Its Background*. London: Faber and Faber, 1970.

Ricoeur, Paul. "The Metaphorical Process as Cognition, Imagination, and Feeling." Sacks, *On Metaphor* 141–57.

Rodríguez, Ileana, and Marc Zimmerman, eds. *Process of Unity in Caribbean Society: Ideologies and Literature*. Minneapolis: Institute for the Study of Ideologies and Literature, 1983.

Rodríguez Monegal, Emir. *El "Boom" de la novela latinoamericana*. Caracas: Editorial Tiempo Nuevo, 1972.

————. "La narrativa hispanoamericana. Hacia una nueva 'poética.'" *Teoría de la novela*. Ed. Santos Sanz Villanueva and Carlos J. Barbachano. Madrid: Sociedad General Española, 1976. 171–206.

————. "Lo real y lo maravilloso en *El reino de este mundo*." Müller-Bergh, *Asedios a Alejo Carpentier* 101–32.

————. "Realismo mágico vs. literatura fantástica: un diálogo de sordos." Yates, *Otros mundos otros fuegos* 25–37.

Roget, Wilbert J. "The Image of Africa in the Writings of Edouard Glissant." *College Language Association* 21 (1978): 390–99.

————. "Land and Myth in the Writings of Edouard Glissant." *World Literature Today* 63.4 (1989): 626–31.

Rohlehr, Gordon. "The Problem of the Problem of Form: The Idea of an Aesthetic Continuum and Aesthetic Code-switching in West Indian Literature." *Caribbean Quarterly* 31 (March 1985): 1–52.

Sacks, Sheldon, ed. *On Metaphor*. Chicago: University of Chicago Press, 1978.

Said, Edward. *Beginnings: Intention and Method*. New York: Columbia University Press, 1985.

————. *The World, the Text, and the Critic*. Cambridge, Mass.: Harvard University Press, 1983.

Schwarz-Bart, Simone. *Pluie et vent sur Télumée Miracle*. Paris: Seuil, 1972. Trans. and intro. Bridget Jones, *The Bridge of Beyond*. London: Heinemann, 1982.

————. *Ti Jean L'horizon*. Paris: Seuil, 1979. Trans. Barbara Bray, *Between Two Worlds*. New York: Harper and Row, 1981.

Sebeok, Thomas A., ed. *Myth: A Symposium*. Bloomington: Indiana University Press, 1974.

Silinieks, Juris. "Glissant's Prophetic Vision of the Past." *African Literature Today* 11 (1980): 161–67.

————. "The Maroon Figure in Caribbean Francophone Prose." Luis, *Voices from Under* 115–25.

Silva Cáceres, Raul. "Una novela de Carpentier." *Mundo Nuevo* 17 (1967): 33–37.

Skinner, Eugene Raymond. "Archetypal Patterns in Four Novels of Alejo Carpentier." Ph.D. diss., University of Kansas, 1969.

Slochower, Harry. *Mythopoesis: Mythic Patterns in the Literary Classics*. Detroit, Mich.: Wayne State University Press, 1970.

Spengler, Oswald. *The Decline of the West*. Trans. Charles Francis Atkinson. New York: Alfred A. Knopf, 1926.

Sypher, Wylie. *Rococo to Cubism in Art and Literature*. New York: Vintage Books, 1960.

Tagliacozzo, Giorgio, and Hayden V. White, eds. *Vico: An International Symposium*. Baltimore: Johns Hopkins University Press, 1969.

Taylor, Patrick. *The Narrative of Liberation: Perspectives on Afro-Caribbean Literature, Popular Culture, and Politics*. Ithaca, N.Y. and London: Cornell University Press, 1989.

Todorov, Tzvetan. *The Conquest of America*. Trans. Richard Howard. New York: Harper, 1985.

Underhill, Evelyn. *Mysticism*. New York: New American Library, 1974.

Uslar Pietri, Alonso. "The Mestizo Experience and the New World." *New Writings in the Caribbean: Carifesta '72*. Ed. A. J. Seymour. [Georgetown?] Guyana: Guyana Lithographic Co. Ltd., 1972. 172–78.

Van Gennep, Arnold. *Rites of Passage*. Trans. Monika B. Vizedom and Gabrielle L. Coffe. Chicago: University of Chicago Press, 1966.

Vickery, John B., ed. *Myth and Literature: Contemporary Theory and Practice*. Lincoln: University of Nebraska Press, 1966.

Vico, Giambattista. *The New Science*. 3d. ed. Trans. Thomas Goddard Bergin and Max Fisch. Ithaca, N.Y.: Cornell University Press, 1968.

Walcott, Derek. "The Muse of History." Baugh, *Critics on Caribbean Literature* 38–43.

Wehr, Demaris S. *Jung and Feminism: Liberating Archetypes*. Boston: Beacon Press, 1987.

White, Hayden. *Metahistory*. Baltimore: Johns Hopkins University Press, 1973.

————. *Tropics of Discourse*. Baltimore: Johns Hopkins University Press, 1978.

Williams, Eric. *From Columbus to Castro: The History of the Caribbean, 1492–1969*. New York: Harper and Row, 1970.

Williams, Lorna V. "The Utopian Vision in Carpentier's *El reino de este mundo.*" *Journal of Caribbean Studies* 2 (1981): 129–39.

World Literature Today. Edouard Glissant Issue. 63.4 (1989).

Yates, Donald, ed. *Otros mundos otros fuegos: fantasía y realismo mágico en Iberoamérica.* Memoria del XVI Congreso Internacional de Literatura Iberoamericana. Pittsburgh: A publication of the Latin American Studies Center of Michigan State University, 1975.

Yates, Frances A. *The Art of Memory.* Chicago: University of Chicago Press, 1966.

Yoder, Lauren W. "A Caribcentric View of the World: The Novels of Edouard Glissant." *Caribbean Review* 10 (1981): 24–27.

Index

183